I am praying that *Mission Accomplished* will be mightily used of God to extend his kingdom internationally.

At whatever stage you're in of your journey to know God and to make him known, this remarkable, easy-to-read book will inform, inspire, encourage, and challenge you. I give it my highest recommendation.

JOY DAWSON
Missionary, International Bible Teacher, Author
Sunland, California

Mission Accomplished clearly helps the reader identify their purpose and calling, while living a passionate and fulfilling life for Christ. I wish this book had been around when I first got saved because it clearly lays out what life can be like while living in obedience to Jesus. Marty's descriptive testimonies reveal the radical love that God has for each and every one of us. *Mission Accomplished* is loaded with truth that will keep you from a life of mediocrity. Marty was truly led by the Holy Spirit as he wrote this inspiring and life-changing manuscript about living in God's fullness.

JIM DURAN
Lead Pastor, The River Community Forsquare Church
Ventura, California

Mission Accomplished offers believers a clear, powerful, compelling call to discover the fullness of their destiny and calling in Jesus Christ. Stories and Scripture illustrate how to align our lives with God's unique design for us.

Dr. Marty Meyer exudes the joy that comes from spreading the Good News vividly, inviting readers to discover and experience this thrill for themselves. This book will rekindle your own passion and get you refocused!

LIZ ADLETA
Global Prayer Strategist serving the Ethne Movement
and the 24:14 Coalition
Fairview, Texas

Mission Accomplished is the most edifying and significant book I have read on the Great Commission in particular or missiology in general. Dr. Meyer has written from a lifetime of experience in many nations, as one of Jesus' "sent ones" under fascinating and sometimes dangerous conditions.

With infectious joy, this book is about the Father's intention and calling of every believer to meld together Jesus' Great Commandment and Great Commission into a single flow of life, making a difference in a broken world.

Having been involved directly in mission work in India and the Middle East for nearly thirty years, I found myself acquiring new insights into what makes following Jesus attractive and desirable, even among people opposed to the Gospel. Marty's approach is uniquely significant among the abundant literature on missiology. I predict it will become a classic resource on the scope of a comprehensive Christian life based on the importance of these two great commandments.

REV. DR. DONALD G. MILES
President Emeritus, India Transformed!
Denver, Colorado

Marty Meyer has quite a story to tell! His *Mission Accomplished* is a compelling, stirring account, including reflection on relevant scripture passages illustrated by gripping, personally lived-out experiences from his life as a missionary. Reading it will indeed help many discover their unique destinies in Jesus Christ's call, to follow him in the particular mission he has for each of us. What an adventurous, thrilling way to live our brief lives on earth—serving with all our hearts the One who created and redeemed us, and empowers us day by day to make a difference in his global purposes! You will want not only to read it yourself, but also to discuss with others the thoughtful questions at the end of each chapter.

JOHN ROBB
Chairman, International Prayer Council
Albuquerque, New Mexico

Dr. Marty Meyer has delivered another powerful book filled with page-turning, real life illustrations, along with a solid biblical foundation, as he calls believers to walk in the calling and purpose God has for them. You will find yourself, and those you disciple, inspired and challenged to step out in faith and obey Jesus fully.

ROD ENOS
Lead Pastor, Southside Christian Center
Meridian, Idaho

We have inherent purpose rather than a purpose we must create and sustain. Thankfully, we are given purpose in Christ to be who he has made us to be. And that purpose is lived out in his Great Commandment and Great Commission. If you want to be inspired in this purpose that God gave you, then *Mission Accomplished* is a "must read." Warning! Be prepared to have your purpose re-ignited!

DR. ROGER THEIMER

Founder, Kids Kount Ministries and Kids Kount India
Omaha, Nebraska

In *Mission Accomplished*, Dr. Marty Meyer weaves a great tale of personal vignettes and hard-core theological points about mission. With an affable style, Marty shares stories that are sure to instruct and inspire people as he opens eyes to the rationale for world mission, woven together with practical steps to understand what to do and how to get involved.

BISHOP BILL ATWOOD

Anglican Bishop, Ambassador for the fifty million-member
GAFCON Movement
Frisco, Texas

Imagine you just finished the great race of life and you hear loud cheers from the throngs of heaven as YOUR name is called. Imagine JESUS walking up to YOU with a crown saying, "Well done, thou good and faithful servant." You will have the joy of a mission accomplished.

This book will ruin you for the ordinary and reveal God's perfect design for your life. I have known Marty and Kelly for years; they are the real deal. This book is a masterpiece of clear, simple instructions to align your life with God's plan.

DAVE GUSTAVESON

Director, YWAM Global Target Network,
Discipleship Training Course
Castle Rock, Colorado

What if God began to use you to touch people in the darkest, most challenging places on earth? What might happen if your heart was filled with an unquenchable love for those without Christ and without hope? It that even possible?

Mission Accomplished provides tangible answers to these and other questions as we learn how God uses ordinary followers of Christ for extraordinary impact. If I could give one gift with potential to help you become a full partner in God's mission, it would be *Mission Accomplished!* I believe God will use this to transform your life, your family, your church and your world!

TOM VICTOR
President, The Great Commission Coalition
Kingwood, Texas

Marty Meyer has written a must-read book on missions. I've known Marty for over a decade now and have seen him in action in multiple nations. His book flows from who he really is. It is Bible centered, full of real life stories intended to help you reflect and re-align your heart towards God's purposes for your life.

I highly recommend reading it, to be inspired and find your fit in God's world.

ALDRIN BOGI
Executive Director, Biblica — The International Bible Society
South Asia

mission accomplished

DISCOVER YOUR DESTINY IN THE MISSION OF JESUS

MARTY MEYER

YWAM Publishing

Seattle, Washington

YWAM Publishing is the publishing ministry of Youth With A Mission (YWAM), an international missionary organization of Christians from many denominations dedicated to presenting Jesus Christ to this generation. To this end, YWAM has focused its efforts in three main areas: (1) training and equipping believers for their part in fulfilling the Great Commission (Matthew 28:19), (2) personal evangelism, and (3) mercy ministry (medical and relief work).

For a free catalog of books and materials, call (425) 771-1153 or (800) 922-2143. Visit us online at www.ywampublishing.com.

Mission Accomplished: Discover Your Destiny in the Mission of Jesus
Copyright © 2018 by Dr. Marty Meyer

Published by YWAM Publishing
a ministry of Youth With A Mission
P.O. Box 55787, Seattle, WA 98155-0787

ISBN 978-1-57658-959-5

Dedication

This book is dedicated to our faithful team of financial supporters. Your sacrificial, consistent giving over the past twenty-five years has enabled our family to serve as full-time missionaries for the purpose of the Great Commission. Countless people have invested in special projects and outreach trips that continue to yield fruit for God's kingdom. Your gifts and prayers have sent us to the ends of the earth, and empowered us to disciple and multiply workers into the harvest field. The stories in this book are fueled by your steadfast partnership. We are humbled, and immensely grateful. You know who you are. We love you!

— Marty & Kelly

Acknowledgements

Mission Accomplished was a team effort. The writing is a reflection of the excellent and diligent work of my primary editor, Chard Berndt. I am also grateful for the insightful refinements in editing by my wife, Kelly, and the final proofing expertise of our friend, Marcia Zimmerman. Thank you, each one of you, for your dedication and persistence to see this project well-completed.

The greatest credit goes to my best friend, Jesus, who taught me to listen to his voice and walk in obedience, to the Holy Spirit who empowered me through extended periods of writing and provided inspirational ideas and structure for this book, and to my Father who continually instills identity, so that his approval is the only one that matters. Until I see the King face-to-face, may I live fully to bring glory to his name!

About the Cover

The ultimate goal of missions is found in every people group worshiping God. In Revelation 7:9 we get a glimpse of this worshipful gathering:

> After this I looked and there before me was a great multitude that no one could count, from every nation, tribe, people and language, standing before the throne and in front of the Lamb. They were wearing white robes and were holding palm branches in their hands.

In this artist's rendition, the vast array of peoples, cultures, colors and dress are represented by hands outstretched in worship. They have grown out every nation to form a single tree that stands in praise of the Creator. Isaiah 55:12 conveys similar imagery—trees clapping their hands together in praise to God.

God's epic Bible story begins with a tree of life in the Garden of Eden and ends with the tree of life in the city of God.

> Then the angel showed me the river of the water of life, as clear as crystal, flowing from the throne of God and of the Lamb down the middle of the great street of the city. On each side of the river stood the tree of life, bearing twelve crops of fruit, yielding its fruit every month. And the leaves of the tree are for the healing of the nations. (Rev. 22:1-2)

Included in the "leaves" of this tree is the ancient symbol known as the "healer's hand." An important aspect of missions is found in redeeming cultures. As people from around the globe find and follow the Savior, Jesus Christ, they bring their distinctive cultural identities and are grafted into a beautiful tree, blossoming in worship to the one true God.

Contents

Foreword

As with his previous book, *Epic Faith*, Marty Meyer has once again left no stone unturned in delivering a potent and clear challenge to "Epic Missions" in *Mission Accomplished*. Drawing on all he has learned from his own missionary experience and leadership over the last twenty-five years, he has laid out a clear pathway to seeing the mission—the Great Commission—completed.

As I read the manuscript, I was reminded of the Apostle Paul's "Golden Chain of Redemption" (Rom. 8:29-30) in which he wrote of those God "has glorified" in the past tense, as if it had already happened, when in reality it is yet to be accomplished. This is why *Mission Accomplished* provides such an appropriate sequel to *Epic Faith*, in which Marty follows the writer of Hebrews in defining present faith as "the substance of things hoped for" in the future (Heb. 11:1).

Likewise in eighteen short faith-filled chapters, Marty has given us practical and biblical pathways to applying epic faith in the present, all the while keeping within our future vision that great and glorious day when in reality the mission *will* be accomplished. Much like the pieces of a puzzle that require the box top to complete the big picture, these chapters, which could be taken individually as daily devotionals, are more faith-building when taken in the context of the accomplished mission, which Marty skillfully weaves through the entire book.

So, get ready, dear reader, for a fast-moving ride on this train which is bound for glory and, as the song says, "...you don't need no ticket, you just get on board," as we join with the growing army of faith-filled spiritual warriors sold out to see the Great Commission accomplished.

Danny Lehmann
International Dean, College of Christian Ministries
University of The Nations

Introduction

This is a call for every believer to discover the destiny for which they were created. This is a charge to find your purpose fulfilled by taking your rightful place in the completion of the Great Commission. This is an opportunity to discover that living out Jesus' final mandate is *the key* to living your life with purpose and joy.

If you regard this as an overstatement, let me ask you some questions: Do you ever feel as if your life lacks purpose? Do you wonder if you were created to play a role in a plot more extensive than your individual story? Do you ever read the Bible and sense a nagging suspicion that you might be missing something? Do you see a discrepancy between your life and the faith and purpose of the early Christ-followers found in Scripture?

If you find yourself answering yes to any of the questions above, let me ask you one more. On a scale from one to ten, to what degree has the purpose of your life been linked to the fulfillment of the Great Commission? Jesus gave a final mandate to all who would call themselves Christ followers; to share his Good News and make disciples, who then themselves make disciples, until all the peoples of earth have heard how to be reconciled to the Father. This is the most meaningful and fulfilling purpose with which any church or individual follower of Jesus could align. If you gave yourself a low score on the question above, I have some good news for you. You are about to experience a "purpose revival" that will dramatically impact your life!

We all long for that day when the Master says, "Well done, good and faithful servant!" (Matt. 25:21a) Those words are based on what we have done with what we have been given. In context, Jesus tells a story to make a very specific point. (The story is found in Matt. 25:14–46.) The master, representing God, gives each of his servants something to steward. A talent. An entrustment. The master departs but expects his servants to be faithful with what they've been given. When the master returns, those servants who were faithful with the entrusted gift were awarded with these words:

> His master replied, "Well done, good and faithful servant! You
> have been faithful with a few things; I will put you in charge
> of many things. Come and share your master's happiness!"
> (Matt. 25:21)

Jesus also had a stern rebuke for the one who was not a good steward.

So, the question is, have we been obedient and faithful with what Jesus has entrusted to us? We want to be certain of the answer to that question because Jesus' reward at the end of our life is based on our faithfulness to his commands. I am not inferring works righteousness, but Jesus clearly promises heavenly rewards for those who obey. The Bible does not specify what those rewards will be, but knowing Jesus, they will be fantastic! Obedience to Jesus not only provides a future benefit, but the joy and fulfillment that we experience in this life is directly related to our faithful stewardship of what he has entrusted to us. In Jesus' summation to this story he said:

"When the Son of Man comes in his glory, and all the angels with him, he will sit on his throne in heavenly glory. All the nations will be gathered before him..." (Matt. 25:31-32) Discovering that your faithfulness to his commands will have a direct connection to this ingathering of the nations is significant!

It may sound like an oversimplification, but we can summarize all of God's commands in just two directives: The Great Commandment and the Great Commission.

When asked what the greatest commandment was, Jesus replied, "'Love the Lord your God with all your heart and with all your soul and with all your mind.' This is the first and greatest commandment. And the second is like it: 'Love your neighbor as yourself.' All the Law and the Prophets hang on these two commandments." (Matt. 22:37-40)

The word that Jesus used for "love" in this passage is *agapao*, which means a commitment of devotion that is directed by the will. We get to choose to love God! It's not a flighty falling in love, but a willful life-decision we make. Jesus is very clear about how we express our love to God. "If you love me, you will obey what I command." (John 14:15)

Please understand that we are not talking about earning salvation through obedience. Salvation comes only as a gift from the Father through the sacrifice of his Son. We are talking rather about our response to that love, that grace, causing us to live our lives in devotion to him. The root of our problem, leading to purposeless lives, is that we have made faith all about the end goal of future salvation, when the Father desires a vibrant daily relationship with his sons and daughters.

Our narrow focus on how we can get into heaven has kept us from seeing that getting saved is just the beginning of the journey—the Father has so much more in store for us. Salvation is the starting place, and it's high time we discover our purpose! Eternal life starts now, and is filled with purpose and adventure as we walk in obedience to his commands.

So what are those commands? According to Jesus, the summation of all the law and the prophets is to love God and to love others. Jesus refers to a scripture that would have been very familiar to his listeners:

> Love GOD, your God, with your whole heart: love him with all that's in you, love him with all you've got!
>
> Write these commandments that I've given you today on your hearts. Get them inside of you and then get them inside your children. Talk about them wherever you are, sitting at home or walking in the street; talk about them from the time you get up in the morning to when you fall into bed at night. Tie them on your hands and foreheads as a reminder; inscribe them on the doorposts of your homes and on your city gates. (Deut. 6:5-9 MSG)

I want you to see that Jesus advocates a radical love relationship with God; one so vital that you cannot stop thinking or talking about him. He should occupy our hearts and every waking hour of our days. You can't get enough of God and your purpose is fueled by your radical love for Him! I'm here to tell you that this is the only kind of Christianity that makes any sense at all. Many try to practice a lukewarm Christianity in which they have just enough of God for a ticket to heaven, and then wonder why their lives lack vibrancy. When you follow Jesus wholeheartedly, it leads to a radical love relationship with the Father. Hold on, because he will stretch you to the max and you will be the better for it.

Jesus continues his summation in declaring that it is not enough to love God, we also must love others. The apostle John echoes this truth:

> ...I am not writing you a new command but one we have had from the beginning. I ask that we love one another. And this is love: that we walk in obedience to his commands. As you have heard from the beginning, his command is that you walk in love. (2 John 1:5b-6)

As faithful stewards of the Father's trust, we want to be obedient not only to the Great Commandment, but also to his Great Commission. Jesus gave one final mandate right before he ascended to heaven. This final command (commission) brings the two mandates together into a beautiful harmony.

> Then Jesus came to them and said, "All authority in heaven and on earth has been given to me. Therefore go and make disciples of all nations, baptizing them in the name of the Father and of the Son and of the Holy Spirit, and teaching them to obey everything I have commanded you. And surely I am with you always, to the very end of the age." (Matt. 28:18-20)

We demonstrate our love for God by obedience to his command to share his love to the whole world. We love others by inviting them into a love relationship with the Father.

> This is how much God loved the world: He gave his Son, his one and only Son. And this is why: so that no one need be destroyed; by believing in him, anyone can have a whole and lasting life. God didn't go to all the trouble of sending his Son merely to point an accusing finger, telling the world how bad it was. He came to help, to put the world right again. Anyone who trusts in him is acquitted; anyone who refuses to trust him has long since been under the death sentence without knowing it. And why? Because of that person's failure to believe in the one-of-a-kind Son of God when introduced to him. (John 3:16-18 MSG)

In the Great Commission, God calls us to "go and tell." He gives us the opportunity to demonstrate our love for him through our obedience to share the Good News and make disciples. That includes every person in the whole world.

So, one may ask, in the light of the Great Commandment *and* the Great Commission, *what have I done with what I have been given?* Have I been a faithful steward of all the Father has entrusted to me?

When we engage in practicing the greatest commandment of all, and likewise the greatest commission, our lives are infused with destiny beyond our imagination. You are about to embark on an adventure that will drastically change your life.

Begin by asking some important "what if" questions:

- What if the Great Commission is the most important mandate because Father knows better than anyone that His commission is integrally tied to my destiny?

- What if it's not about God trying to get me to do something that I really don't want to do, but rather that he is opening a door to my most fulfilling life?
- What if my life *can* have purpose?
- What if I can impact another human being and see that person's life changed for eternity?
- What if I was created for something much bigger than myself?

Mission Accomplished will lead you on a journey of discovering the destiny for which you were created. We are going to explore the meaning of the Great Commission and how it is accomplished. Remember, your purpose is connected to its fulfillment. We will seek ways to engage Christ's call in meaningful ways and discover an incredible power with which we can tap into when we are living presently and purposefully with Jesus. Our God-empowered purpose leads to maximum impact, making our actions count both for the moment and for eternity.

As you read, you will notice that I have borrowed a few stories from my former book. *Mission Accomplished* will set your course on a life-fulfilling trajectory and *Epic Faith* will provide inspiration and faith principles for each step of that journey. Continue to nurture your God-focused adventure by reading *Epic Faith* upon completion of this book.

At the end of each chapter you will find the heading "Accomplish It!" This section is designed to cultivate a lifestyle of obedience focused on completing the task. Completing the Great Commission requires all of us taking small steps towards that goal. Here you will find guidance to accomplish it!

I challenge you to read the chapters that follow with an open heart and allow a flame to begin to flicker within you. It is his desire that your heart come alive and your days be filled with meaning and purpose. I pray that your heart will burn with a passion for the name of Jesus to be known and worshiped among every people and language until you hear the words of the Master saying, "Well done, good and faithful servant. Mission accomplished!"

Part 1: Discover Your Destiny in the Mission of Jesus

Our enemy is more aware than we are of the spiritual possibilities that depend upon obedience.

— Amy Carmichael

Chapter 1

Passion for Life

Go into all the world and preach the Good News
to all creation.
— Jesus Christ

I found myself weeping on the floor, enclosed in a small room of a rundown Salvation Army youth hostel in Mumbai, India. The source of my travail was not mere sadness but something much deeper—as if an unfulfilled longing shattered my heart. I didn't understand it, and I couldn't control what was happening to me.

Just hours before, I had experienced one of my life's greatest joys. I had been exploring the streets of Mumbai when I discovered a narrow and seemingly secret passageway that zigzagged through ramshackle buildings and dingy homes until it opened into an expansive fishing village nestled on the shore of the Arabian Sea. Though I could not speak their language, the people welcomed this blond hair blue-eyed 25-year-old American into their community. I watched the old fishermen mend nets, much like I had imagined Peter and Andrew doing prior to being sent out by Jesus for a miraculous catch. When some teenagers started a soccer game on their makeshift field, which incidentally doubled as the community bathroom, I joined in and quickly found myself in the goalkeeper position. The goal I guarded was comprised of two sticks shoved into the dry, rocky soil.

I had been an acclaimed goalie at the university level, and after making a remarkable save, the game quickly changed to "let's take turns trying to score on the American." Something like thirty penalty kicks followed. I dove at shot after shot, soon covered in filth, but I didn't care. To see the laughter and celebration on those teen faces when someone scored against me made the dirt-crusting all worth it. Ultimately I had to say goodbye to my new friends as it was getting late, and I felt certain that my outreach team would be wondering as to where I had disappeared.

Later that evening when I decided to take some time in prayer and reflection, I was overwhelmed with uncontrollable weeping and dropped face-first to the floor. Uncertain what was happening, I began to cry out to God for answers. Am I losing my mind? Why does my heart feel like it's breaking? Does this have something to do with my desire to be a missionary?

Until recently, I hadn't ever considered becoming a missionary. So what had brought me to this place, in a city a world away from my Idaho home?

Missionary Seeds

I grew up unaware of the significance of the Great Commission. I knew that Jesus had instructed his disciples to share the Good News of salvation through his death and resurrection with the whole world, but I certainly did not sense that it had anything to do with *my* life purpose. Perhaps seeds of missions had been planted deep in me that were waiting patiently to grow.

My mom served in the ladies' group at church that intentionally supported foreign missionaries. The women would at times sell baked goods to raise money for missions' projects or would put together a used clothing drive and send a care package to people serving God in some faraway place. Mom must have played a special role in this, because when missionaries visited our church they would present her with "artifacts" such as hand-carved bowls, plates and wooden forks. These gifts were proudly displayed on our family's dining room wall.

From time to time, during family devotions, Mom would tell my siblings and me stories she had heard from missionaries from the field. I still vividly recall one story that was especially scary to a seven-year-old boy. It tells of a man who served as a missionary to a remote tribe of headhunters in the jungles of New Guinea. This westerner discovered an in-road to this unique people by adopting their way of life and eventually becoming one of them—with the exception that he would never join in the raiding and killing of people from other villages. In time he patiently shared the Gospel with this secluded people group, and many in the village became Christians. Even so, some were drawn back to their killing, headhunting ways. Anytime a seeming omen occurred, superstition demanded that the villagers needed another head from the neighboring tribe as a sacrifice. The beloved missionary tried to convince them otherwise, but when he realized that the men would not be dissuaded and more innocent blood would be shed, he offered a solution:

"I happen to know that if you go to this certain place tomorrow night and hide in the bushes along the trail, there will be a man riding on a donkey wearing a red hood. You can take this man as your sacrifice." They did as the missionary had instructed, and as the sun was setting they saw the man approaching on a donkey. The warriors quickly attacked him and cut off his head. As they removed the hood they were shocked to discover that they had just taken the life of their friend—their own beloved missionary.

They realized then that the missionary had willingly given his own life in the place of another, to rescue them from their sinful ways—and that in doing so he was an example of what Jesus had done for them. They were struck to the heart and repented for all the blood they had shed. They honored the fallen missionary with a proper burial and committed to follow Jesus wholeheartedly.

I remember being very disturbed by the story, thinking that this missionary must have made a terrible mistake. Yet I couldn't deny that Jesus had made the same sacrificial, horrifically wonderful choice for us. Before he died on the cross he told his followers, "The reason my Father loves me is that I lay down my life—only to take it up again. No one takes it from me, but I lay it down of my own accord." (John 10:17-18a)

While I was in grade school our church sponsored a refugee family from Vietnam. We learned that this family was well educated yet had nothing since fleeing for their lives from their war-torn country. My mom had volunteered my family to serve as hosts for these new arrivals.

I remember great frustration in not being able to communicate with our Vietnamese guests. I wondered about how lost they certainly felt in a new environment with a completely different culture, food, language and way of life. In time they learned English, the parents secured jobs, the children went to school, and our families became dear friends.

Dad helped to find a small house for them; a tall two-story home, though very narrow and in terrible need of paint. Yan, the mother, wanted to paint it in two tones, but in a way that looked unusual to us. We did as she desired and painted the top half of their house bright green and the bottom half bright yellow. My brother called it "tutti frutti" because it looked like a lemon and a lime smashed together.

Our new Vietnamese family members would often invite us over in appreciation for the things our family did for them. Some of their food was amazing—like nothing I had ever tasted before, in a good way— while other dishes horrified our senses. We secretly called one dessert "green pea under the sea" because it looked like a chartreuse swampy pudding with unknown bits swimming about. I didn't want to offend them, but I could not bring myself to partake of it.

Looking back, I'm grateful for these experiences that exposed me to people of cultures different from my own. It's easy to become so comfortable with our way of life that we ignore the greater world we live in and the implications of the Gospel to reach it. Our comfort becomes a prison that keeps us from the destiny for which we were created. While entire peoples created in God's image still wait to hear the Gospel, our isolation keeps us from bringing it, as well as from receiving the joy of discovering the uniqueness God has deposited in them.

What is the Great Commission?

Why do so many of us find church boring and lack a sense of destiny in our own lives? It's because we have neglected the central purpose to which Jesus has called us.

Just prior to taking his last breath on the cross Jesus cried out in a loud voice, "It is finished." He did what he came to do. He gave his life as a sacrifice for the sins of the whole world. Mission accomplished! But the mission of his disciples, including you and me, was only beginning.

Jesus rose from the dead and gives us this same resurrection power to accomplish his purpose. What purpose? He didn't want us to miss it, so he delineated it through his very last words on earth before ascending to heaven. I quoted this in the Introduction, but let's have a look this important passage again:

> Then Jesus came to them and said, "All authority in heaven and on earth has been given to me. Therefore go and make disciples of all nations, baptizing them in the name of the Father and of the Son and of the Holy Spirit, and teaching them to obey everything I have commanded you. And surely I am with you always, to the very end of the age." (Matt. 28:18-20)

Embedded in these epic words spoken over 2,000 years ago is a key to the life-purpose of each one of us. We commonly refer to this scripture and Jesus' mandate to make disciples of all nations as the "Great Commission." Although Jesus made his assignment painfully clear, many believers fail to recognize that this is *their primary purpose*. More alarming is the fact that most believers are completely unaware of the Great Commission.

A recent Barna study asked regular church-goers if they had ever heard the term, "The Great Commission." While a meager half of those polled had previously heard the phrase, only seventeen percent could explain what it meant. Keep in mind, this is not a survey of people off the street, but of those who identify themselves as Christians who regularly attend church.

Barna also presented churchgoers with five different passages from Scripture and asked them to identify which one is known as the Great Commission. A little more than one-third of churchgoers (37%) correctly identified the Bible passage Matthew 28:18-20.[1]

Equally troubling is the fact that the younger the generation, the less likely they are to identify the Great Commission as found in Scripture. Not only have we failed to embrace the destiny-fulfilling effects of the Great Commission, we have failed to inspire the next generation toward their primary purpose in life! How will we discover passion for life if we are disconnected from our primary purpose? Our disconnect from the Great Commission leaves us wandering aimlessly like the unemployed workers in Jesus' parable of the vineyard.[2] We remain idle and aimless when the master wants to give us meaningful engagement in his vineyard.

Finding Purpose in God's Mission

As a teenager I remained rudderless while searching for direction. The only thing that gave me a sense of purpose was working at a Christian summer camp in the mountains of Idaho. Initially it was all about the fishing, backpacking and mountain climbing. But something began to shift in my heart. Jesus had become more important in my life and I thrived on seeing the "lights come on" among the young campers. Throughout my high school years and into college I would anticipate my summer retreat into Idaho's crags to spend those days impacting young persons with God's Word. I loved working at camp with my brother and my closest friends—it's what I lived for.

My older brother, Rob, was the camp's director and from time to time he would invite his friends with missionary experiences to share with the campers. I remember listening to his friend Jerry with wide-eyed amazement as he told stories of smuggling Bibles into Russia. He was risking his life to take the Bible, a book I took for granted, to people who had never encountered the Word of God.

Other friends, Dan and Cathleen, visited the camp and shared stories of working with Laotian people. Dan gave a testimony of how he had previously hated the Asian culture and had allowed past wounds to build walls of prejudice in him. When Dan and his wife signed up to go on a short-term mission to Australia, God sent them to work with Laotian refugees living there! God changed his heart and they fell in love with these displaced people from the country of Laos.

Toward the end of one of my summers I received a strange prompting. It was as if I knew that I would not be returning to camp the following year. I felt a strong impression that instead of working at camp, I was to go on a mission trip. I did not recognize it at that time as "the voice of God," but looking back it is clear that he was orchestrating a divine encounter that would leave a life-changing impact.

The following season, Dan and Cathleen helped me find a summer-long "Around-the-World Outreach" facilitated through a group called Youth With A Mission out of Los Angeles.

The outreach started with two weeks of missions and evangelism training and the more I learned, the more I became convinced that I wanted to be a missionary. What touched me even more deeply than the teaching was the passion for Jesus evident in the hearts of young missionaries around me. One young man leading worship would pound on the keys and make up lyrics as he went along. I will never forget his passionate prayer, "Lord, I want my heart to break with the things that break yours. I want to be so close to you, Jesus, that I can feel your heart beating inside of me."

By the time I left for outreach, I had two prayers ringing in my *own* heart: "God, where do you want me to go as a missionary?" and "Father, I want to know your heart and feel it beating inside of *me*."

My outreach team traveled to Switzerland, Germany, and France, but it was not until we reached India that the Lord answered both of my prayers. By the time our small team arrived in Mumbai, many of our members fell sick, and some were afraid to go outside our Salvation Army youth hostel to experience Indian culture. So I went out alone, unprepared for the human suffering I witnessed. I observed the sick, the crippled, and the hungry begging for food. I encountered a woman mourning over her husband's dead body in the street. I also discovered that little fishing village by the bay where I began to fall in love with Indian people sewing nets and playing soccer.

As I mentioned before, I had never experienced anything like what suddenly overcame me that evening when I returned to my meager room in the hostel. The next day I convinced two of the guys from my team to go back out into the streets with me. We carried children on our shoulders and played carefree soccer with teenagers, but when I found myself alone later that day, I again fell into inconsolable sobbing. On the third day, when heart-rending tears began to flow, I questioned my sanity and called out to God through my relentless weeping.

"God, what is happening to me? Am I losing my mind? My heart is breaking inside of me and I don't understand why!"

The Lord then spoke to my heart with alarming clarity: "Marty, you have been praying that you might know my heart. I have revealed to you how my heart breaks for my lost children." Even as those words resonated, the Lord began to question me: "Do you think that I do not see those who die in the streets? Do you think that I do not long for those who are separated from me? Who will be my hands and who will be my feet? Who will be my mouthpiece that brings the only message that gives life?"

The tears stopped flowing but my heart pounded, sobered by the seriousness of his questioning. I felt like giving a logical response, but could I muster the courage to pray it? Finally, softly, I spoke, "Here am I, send me. I'll spend the rest of my life as a missionary in India. Just say the word."[3]

Knowing the Father's Heart

This experience of feeling God's heart and my simple prayer of response has shaped the destiny of my life. I have found my true life's purpose, as all believers must, by connecting to God's purpose. One might try to deflect that idea by saying, "Marty, that's just because *you* are *called* to be a missionary." To this, I will simply point out that the Great Commission is not given to some special category of Christian, rather it was mandated to all who would consider himself or herself a follower of Jesus.

Others might retort, "If I had a special experience like Marty had, then certainly I would invest my life in the Great Commission." If this sentiment is sincere, I would invite you to earnestly seek the Father and ask him to give you a revelation of his longing heart for his lost children. This is a prayer Abba loves to answer! I have often prayed with earnest believers to receive an impartation of Father's heart and have observed the overwhelming love of God for the lost fill their heart as he did for me years ago on a dirty youth hostel floor. These earnest God-seekers always emerge from the experience with fresh resolve to impact the nations.

The question is not, "Does Jesus want me to go?" The question is, "Will I ask God to give me his heart for the lost, and persist until I receive it?" When you feel his heart beating inside your chest you will know the answer to that question.

But even if one never receives a special revelation, it does not change the simple truth that the Word of God calls us to go. Anyone who wants to discover real purpose will find it *in connection to* this final command of Jesus: "Go, and make disciples!"

Jesus completed his mission on the cross and gave access to every tribe and people group to come into a reconciled relationship with Father. Our mission is to go and share this Good News with the world, even to the "ends of the earth." The Great Commission is the Father's invitation to join him in a life-transforming adventure. When we say "yes" to him, we discover a course set before us that brings a new level of intimacy with God and a sense of purpose that our heart has been longing for.

This task is far from complete, but it is within reach. It will be accomplished by faithful Christ followers like you and me who hear his call and respond in faith.

Jesus, I want to connect with your call for my life in a meaningful way. I pray that the mission seeds that you have been planting in my heart would spring to life. Father, I want to know you more intimately. Give me an impartation of your heart for your lost children. I want my heart to beat with passion for your purposes. Amen.

Accomplish It!

- What "mission seeds" can you identify in your own life?

- How might your daily life change with a greater alignment to the Great Commission?

- Go online and begin to research famous Christian missionaries. We can learn from and be inspired by those who have gone before us.

- Intentionally cultivate a friendship with a family living near you from a different culture.

Chapter 2

Guidance for the Journey

He is no fool who gives up what he cannot keep
to gain that which he cannot lose.
— Jim Elliot

We landed in Bangkok, Thailand and were bombarded by a whole new array of sights and sounds and smells. Our first stop at the local bustling street market was both a delightful and disturbing assault on my senses. Street venders vocalizing intense tones invited shoppers to purchase fresh fruit, fried squid, or roasted octopus. I already loved Thailand but was confused as to why I was here.

Back in India, while on the floor of my room in that hostel, I had submitted the rest of my life to be a missionary, if God were to only just say the word. I did not understand why Father didn't take me up on my offer right then and there. I was prepared to stay in India and let the team continue on without me, figuring that God would certainly take anyone so willing to remain long-term. When my prayer met with silence, I resolved to accompany my team to the next stop on our around-the-world itinerary.

Upon arrival in Thailand we began to share the Gospel daily with university students. We struck up conversations easily with young scholars eager to practice their English with native speakers. When the dialogue steered toward Jesus, many listened with rapt attention about a loving God of whom they had never heard. To my surprise, I really enjoyed sharing the Gospel in this simple friendship evangelism style.

One evening we had the opportunity to attend a house-church with a group of Thai university students who had recently become believers. The intensity of their worship impressed me as they expressed their love for God through their newly found faith in Jesus. Some of their worship was expressed through familiar English choruses that had been translated into Thai, so our team sang along in English. I had never experienced the beautiful unity of worshipping simultaneously with shared heart and two languages. When they continued to sing a new Thai worship song, I closed my eyes in prayer and was met by what I can only describe as a vision. I began to see myself back at my home church in my assistant pastor role, but with a unique twist; taking my youth group on mission trips. I pictured transforming the summer camp of which I had previously worked, into a "Mission Camp" that guided students on mission outreaches, training them in evangelism. I saw myself equipping adults from our congregation to share their faith in new and meaningful ways. I began to dream of sending some of our young adults abroad as missionaries. It was then that Jesus broke into this mental "movie clip" with a specific word of clarity. "Marty, if you will be faithful to stay, many will be faithful to go in your place." In that moment I recognized my call from God—to mobilize missionaries. Though I was personally willing to go and be a missionary on the field, Jesus was asking if I would be willing instead to stay and send others.

After my around-the-world adventure, I returned to my church as an assistant pastor and began putting into practice the vision that Jesus revealed to me while worshiping him among those Thai believers. My obedient response led to a fulfilling season of fruitfulness in my life.

God Still Speaks

When we open our spiritual ears to God's voice and respond in obedience, Jesus will grant us clarity and direction to lead us into his fulfilling purpose for our lives. I must be honest—prior to this around-the-world outreach, I wasn't convinced that Jesus even wanted to speak to me. Although I had been raised as a believer, I had never been taught that I could discern God's voice. In fact, the opposite was communicated, essentially as "God only speaks through the Bible. If you want to hear from God, read your Bible." But I couldn't deny that some significant communication had taken place between God and myself while I was on outreach, causing my heart to come alive in ways I had never experienced before!

Like John Bunyan's character, Christian, in *Pilgrim's Progress*,[4] God is calling us on a treacherous journey, yet it's rewarding beyond our imagination. We are also invited on a pilgrimage where our faith and resolve will be tested, but Jesus will prove faithful at every turn. This journey will require step-by-step instruction from the Shepherd, but thankfully, that is exactly what he has promised.

Jesus made it clear in his Word that he would always communicate to his children. "My sheep listen to my voice; I know them, and they follow me." (John 10:27) Jesus explained that we would know how to follow him because we would recognize his voice.

Listen and Obey

When we learn to walk in obedience to the Shepherd's voice, it opens up lines of communication to hear his guidance for our journey. When I felt the heart of God pounding inside my chest, I was then willing to obey the Great Commission. "God, I'll do anything. I'll go anywhere. Whatever you ask of me, the answer is *yes!*" It's as if the Father was just waiting for an obedient heart, then he responded in turn, "Now you are ready to receive my direction." By contrast, at times it seems as if we are asking Father to give us guidance first and then *we* decide whether we will follow it. Let's face it; we'd probably each rather maintain ultimate control of our lives. Yet when this is the case, it is actually a gift of God's grace that he withholds his direction until we are first ready to obey, regardless of what he asks of us!

Many believers unconsciously really don't want to hear God's voice. If deep in our hearts we are unwilling to obey, we will simply stop listening, and falsely credit God with the communicational breakdown. We may even create a theology that says, "God no longer speaks" to get us off the hook for the rebellious disobedience residing hidden in our hearts. Hard to stomach? I know, I've been there.

God is Trustworthy

This reluctance to obey may point to a deeper issue. Do we actually trust God?

My wife Kelly and I have always cherished our friendship with author and international Bible teacher, Joy Dawson,[5] and her late husband, Jim. What has always impressed us about Joy is her unwavering and passionate obedience to the King. She speaks as one who receives her instructions directly from God. It inspires me to emulate that in my own life. Joy constantly directs her focus on the character of God as the reason for her ability to absolutely trust him. Joy states in *The Character of the One Who Says "Go"*,

Because (God) alone has the knowledge of all that's knowable, we can be absolutely secure in the fact that He knows what is best for us at all times. I have proved hundreds of times that I don't know what is best for me. But when I seek God for directions, receive and obey them, I always discover that God has my best interest at heart. The One who created us knows how to completely fulfill us.

His plans for our lives will match our temperament, our natural gifts, and the ministries He wants to give us. He knows our strengths and weaknesses and will team us with people to balance them. He not only knows the plans that will fulfill us the most, but how and when to reveal them.[6]

When we truly trust that God is unmistakably good and that his plan for our lives is unquestionably supreme, we surrender the control to which we grasp so tightly and open up to the direction he intends to provide. Jesus wants to include you in his story. He desires to invite you into the adventure for which you were created. He is waiting for you to listen with an obedient heart.

Six years beyond that transformational around-the-world trip I had faithfully implemented each component of ministry that Jesus had shown me in Thailand. Not only had I led my youth group on annual mission trips, we were also sending cross-cultural outreaches through our camp ministry. I had written a curriculum to equip adults to share the Gospel and many were leading their friends to Christ. We began to see some of our high school graduates head to Bible colleges to prepare for full-time ministry. Meanwhile, I discovered the fulfillment that flowed from being faithful to God's vision and direction for my life. I was poised to receive the next steps from the Father in learning to listen to his voice, but the question remained, would I again obey?

Learning to Listen

I walked to the park down the street from my house, a place I often went to study my Bible. I welcomed the fresh air and warm spring sunshine after a lengthy, cold Pocatello winter.

Several months prior, I had served on an organizational committee of local church leaders that would partner with Youth With A Mission (YWAM) to bring a huge campaign to our area. As a committee member I was given a copy of the book *Is that Really You, God?* by Loren Cunningham, the founder of YWAM. In it Loren tells the story of his life and the birth of this evangelistic organization (which has grown into one of the largest mission agencies in the world). His book was sprinkled with examples of hearing from God and taking steps of obedience, regardless of how audacious the voice of God seemed.

I was unfamiliar with such a personal approach to following the voice of God. Although I thought I had heard the Lord's voice several times in the past, my experiences were hardly like those as expressed by Cunningham. Perhaps because of my go-for-it personality, I came away from finishing the book thinking, *If God speaks to this Loren fellow, then certainly he can speak to me!*

So I had walked down to the park this day, with my mind set on testing this "hearing from God" business for myself. I spent time reading a few Psalms and Proverbs and preparing my heart in prayer. Finally, I began to talk to God. "Jesus, I know that you hear me when I pray, but lately I've been convicted that I don't really expect to hear back from you. I know that you speak to me through the Bible, but I'd like to hear your voice. I want that kind of relationship with you in which you tell me what's on your heart. If there is anything that you'd like to say to me, I pray that you would speak to my heart now."

Almost before I could finish the last word, a whisper emerged in my heart and formed words in my mind, similar to the sensation of an extremely vivid idea.

"Quit your jobs, sell your house, and go to a land I will show you."

The voice seemed firm, yet peaceful. But the content of the message slammed hard against my own voice of reason: This could not possibly be the voice of God! My wife has an excellent, well-paying teaching position and I'm a youth pastor. Jesus would never ask a minister to quit his job!

We were quite comfortable. We often talked about Grace Church as being like our family, where we would raise our future children and grow old together. Pastor Manfred had become like a father to me and had even expressed his desire that I take over his position at Grace when he retired. Everything seemed to be laid out perfectly. Clearly, this mysterious voice I heard in the park did not fit with our secure and well-ordered plans.

Well, that certainly didn't work, I thought with regard to my little experiment in hearing God's voice. I tried to dismiss it altogether, but it kept bugging me like an itch on the back that you can't quite reach. I finally confronted the nagging feeling. *Lord, I really wanted to hear your voice. How could you have let me down?* I decided I would give it one more try the next day. I recalled that Loren Cunningham cautioned in his book that we should "take authority over the devil" when attempting to listen to the voice of God. *That's it,* I thought. *The devil was trying to distract me with that "quit your job" matter.* I would not let that happen again.

The next day I approached my quiet time in the park with renewed confidence. I took my seat atop a particular picnic table, and, after perusing some of my favorite scriptures, I resolved to listen to God. But first I remembered to take authority over the enemy: "In Jesus' name I bind the devil," I began. "Satan, you have no right or authority to speak to me, so I silence you in Jesus' name. I invite God's presence here now, and there is no space allowed for the enemy." A peace settled over me as a gentle breeze rustled budding branches overhead. Not wanting to disturb the moment, I whispered my prayer to God, "Lord, what do you want to say to me?"

The response slammed my mind with alarming clarity: "Quit your jobs, sell your house, and go to a land I will show you."

Though not audible, the voice materialized no less tangibly than actual conversation, no less real than the roughness of the wood I sat upon. The candid moment stunned me—the consideration that the Lord might actually be speaking…and to me! I remained still, trying to make sense of what I had heard, requesting confirmation. Silence lingered.

I hadn't bothered to tell Kelly about my experimental fiasco from the previous day, but now I couldn't ignore or deny that something was happening during my devotional time with Jesus, though I was not yet sure what. The conundrum distracted me the rest of that day: How would I tell Kelly about this? Would she think I was crazy?

Waiting for Kelly to return home from work, I was reminded of that familiar Bible story about Samuel hearing God's voice for the first time. He did not understand it was God speaking until receiving assurance from Eli the priest along with the instruction, "If you hear the voice calling your name again, simply say, 'Speak, for your servant is listening.'" Even Samuel, who became a great man of God, had to *learn* to recognize the voice of God.

The familiar sound of Kelly's Chevy Citation grinding to a halt in our driveway cut my musing short. The moment she walked in the door, book bags slung over both shoulders, Kelly instinctively knew that something was troubling me. She sat down next to me on our denim couch as I struggled to express my thoughts: "You know how I've been reading that book and thinking a lot about this idea of hearing God's voice?" I began. She listened patiently as I recounted my conversations with God over the past two mornings. I had been so reluctant to say the words that I could barely get them out of my mouth. "I mean, could it really be the Lord? What if Jesus is telling us to quit our jobs, sell our house, and go to the place he will show us?"

Kelly's response shook me and revealed the character of the woman God had chosen for me. "Well, one thing's for certain," she said, "if that really is the voice of God, then we will need to obey it."

Even as she spoke the words, I partnered with practical truth rising from deep within. I had been preaching about putting the Word of God into practice. Why should this be any different? If this was the voice of God, we needed to be no less obedient to it. But there was still that bothersome, lingering *if*. How could I be certain that the Lord was really speaking to me?

Somewhere in the quiet, later that sleepless night, an idea occurred to me. I had always trusted the Bible, even as a child in Sunday school—I had no doubt that the Bible was the Word of God. In high school Jesus became my best friend as he revealed himself through the stories recorded in the Gospels. While in Bible college Jesus taught me that he was the real teacher as he illuminated truth from his Word. I drifted off to sleep in peace, knowing what I must do in the morning.

As soon as Kelly went out the door and off to work, I strode down to the park by the early morning light. I tugged at my light jacket, the sun not yet warming the chilly air. My right hand gripped a well-worn leather study Bible, my faithful companion since college days. Finding my perch atop the picnic table under a massive oak tree, I felt an unexpected excitement. This time I was ready.

"Okay, Lord," I said matter-of-factly, meaning it was serious business-time with God. "I take authority over the enemy and silence his voice. I believe that you can talk to me so I invite you to speak, for your servant is listening."

Again the voice, now becoming more familiar, resonated in my heart. "Quit your jobs, sell your house, and go to a land I will show you."

My response revealed my expectation that he would say this same thing again. "Lord, if that's really you, we are willing to obey. But Jesus, I need to be *sure* that it is you. You know that I trust this book." I clenched my Bible and thrust it above my shoulder as if Jesus needed some visual aid to understand my speech. "You have always spoken to me through your Word. Now, if this is really your voice, I want you to say the same thing to me through the Bible."

My prayer was confident, but looking back, I'm not really sure what I expected to happen. I had never before experienced what happened next. I closed my eyes and waited patiently. Without warning, a Bible reference appeared in my mind's eye.

"Genesis 12:1-3."

This impression came as vividly and with the same firm peace I had sensed before. Still, my fingers trembled as I turned pages to the scripture I felt I was being directed to. I had no recollection of what I would find in this passage. My heart skipped a beat as I read the first verse:

The Lord had said to Abram, "Leave your country, your people and your father's household and go to the land I will show you."

I sat suspended in time as the reality of what had just happened sunk in. The Lord had clearly said the same thing to me through his Word, just as I had requested. I was stunned. What would this mean for us? My mind reeled with the ways our lives would radically change, yet I felt sure of one thing: this was God's voice and we would obey it.[7]

Guidance for *Your* Journey

Kelly and I were obedient to the voice of God. We quit our jobs, sold our house and embarked on an adventure with Jesus that continues to this day. You can read that full story with more context in *Epic Faith*, but more importantly, God is wanting to write his story through your life. Simply being obedient to the next thing God shows you to do will set the course for your future with him. Approaching Jesus with ready obedience will prepare you to hear his voice and unlock your destiny.

Hearing God's voice is not just for big-picture life direction, but for tangible daily intimacy the Father wants to enjoy with his children. I set out on prayer walks with Jesus every day, and at some point during our strolls together I ask the simple question, "Jesus, what do you want to say to me today?" Every time, he gives a word of encouragement, an affirmation, or a specific piece of guidance for that day. It's a highlight of my day! The more we cultivate daily listening in the small things, the better we can discern his voice regarding the major steps of faith he may also call us to take. The greater the intimacy, the greater our trust will be to respond in faith.

God's Word makes our primary purpose painfully clear.

He said to them, "Go into all the world and preach the Good News to all creation. Whoever believes and is baptized will be saved, but whoever does not believe will be condemned..." (Mark 16:15-16)

So, whether he calls you to "go" or to "stay and send," you can trust him. The real question is, will you obey, regardless of what he calls you to do? Remember, you can trust the character of God; his plan for your life is ultimately the best and the most fulfilling. God's Word sets the course and his voice gives the specific direction. "In his heart a man plans his course, but the LORD determines his steps." (Proverbs 16:9)

We will always find the greatest satisfaction by aligning our lives to the Great Commission. Listening to his voice will help us personally discern specific steps he has for us to carry out this global purpose. God's call on your life is uniquely woven into the way he created you. Trust him, listen to his voice, respond in obedience, and you will find yourself in a story far beyond yourself.

Father, I'm listening. I want to hear your voice in the quiet of my heart. I believe you have direction that will breathe purpose to my being. I confess the fear that sometimes cripples me. Jesus, give me the courage to say yes to whatever direction you bring. I trust you and know that your plan is absolutely the best for my life. I invite you to speak to me now the next step, big or small, you want me to take....

Accomplish It!

- What could you do to cultivate a lifestyle of listening to the Shepherd's voice?

- With which areas of your life do you find it difficult to fully trust God?

- Have you ever surrendered your heart and life to obedience to Jesus regardless of what he requires? If not, what is holding you back?

- Is there a step you have already felt prompted to take but have delayed? Ask Jesus for the courage to take it now.

- Invite Jesus to speak to you today and be watchful for his reply.

Chapter 3

Motives of the Heart

*May the Lamb that was slain receive
the reward of His suffering!*
— John Dober and David Nitschman

By the time our team returned to Los Angeles from our summer of missions, we had circumnavigated the globe and shared the Gospel with thousands of people in nearly a dozen countries. Each place we visited, I asked Jesus if he wanted me to remain or to return there long-term as a missionary. Surprisingly, he sent me home with a newfound purpose and a single phrase ringing in my heart like a battle cry: "*Raise up an end-time army to complete the Great Commission!*" When you surrender your heart to Jesus he will place within you a purpose and calling, perfectly suited to you.

I can remember the descent into our tiny airport in Pocatello, Idaho. The surroundings looked familiar but something had changed. Merely ten weeks after my departure, I felt like I returned as a different person, my heart eager to make an impact. God had deposited something of his heart into mine.

To my surprise, my church had staged a welcome home celebration in the diminutive terminal. Youth group members held a large "Welcome Home Missionary Marty" banner and everyone held a balloon—even Pastor Manfred, who smiled broadly as he gave me a big squeeze. He shocked me with his whispered request, "How about preaching next Sunday? I know everyone will be excited to hear all about your trip."

"Uh, okay...sure...that would be great," I stammered, obviously taken off guard by his mid-hug offer.

On such short notice, I decided to prepare a message called, "The Father's Broken Heart for a Lost World," since that theme had impacted me most during my outreach. I worked hard that week prepping for what I expected to emerge as a grand sermon replete with scriptures about the Great Commission and, more importantly, communicating how Father God longs for his children that do not know him yet and have no opportunity to hear of his love.

Sunday morning arrived and at the appropriate time, I stepped up to the front. Our traditionally styled church featured a grand wood-carved pulpit, and all eyes fell on me as I stepped into it, its sculpted oak wrapping around me. At first I shared a few interesting stories from various places we had stopped to preach the Gospel. But when I began to speak about India, and how the Father revealed to me his broken heart for his lost children, something totally unexpected happened. Overwhelmed by Father's loving longing heart for the lost, I began to weep just as I had done on the floor of the Salvation Army hostel in Mumbai. Previously when this lament had overtaken me in India, I experienced it alone. No one had witnessed my heart-wrenching wailing, tears streaming down my face, snot pouring from my nose. This time however, I found myself in front of the entire congregation encased in a wooden pulpit, which now propped me up as I clung to it for dear life.

I forced the thought, *Marty, pull it together, this is embarrassing...* but the harder I fought the emotion, the greater it drove me—it would have been easier to stop a runaway train than to put the brakes on this Spirit-driven momentum of God's heartbeat. Finally I succumbed and allowed my heart its only appropriate expression when experiencing the Father's heart for his lost children—inconsolable sobbing. The overflow continued for more than twenty minutes as the Spirit of God translated and channeled the Father's infinite heart through my finite human vessel.

Finally, as the sensation subsided, I regained composure and spoke through saturated eyes. "What you have witnessed this morning is Father's broken heart for his lost children. He is calling us, the people of God, to go and share the only message that brings life to a broken world. Who will go? Who will be his hands and feet? Who will be the voice of Jesus to a lost and hurting world? Jesus came to show us the way to the Father. The time is now to show this way to those who have never heard."

As I delivered this conclusion to my "sermon" through blurred vision it appeared as if no one remained in the pews. Had everyone escaped the sanctuary during my impassioned lament? I mopped my eyes for a more accurate observation, only to discover indeed few were sitting in the pews, because the vast majority was either kneeling or lying face down on the carpet. Some were praying while others were softly weeping, all apparently moved by the same Spirit of God that had gushed through my own heart.

Something remarkable had taken place not only in me, but in each one present, evidenced as we began to work together in the coming months with new resolve to reach the lost. We felt the Father's heart thumping in our chests, transforming our view of the Great Commission mandate.

What are our motivations to complete God's mission? What will sustain a lifetime of passionate service to the King? Since each person's role in the fulfillment of the Great Commission emerges as the greatest life-purpose to which one can align, it would be worthwhile to check our heart motives toward accomplishing this task.

I have discerned seven biblical motivations that fuel participation in the Great Commission. But before I delineate these, I want to encourage you not to stress out about the possibility of reaching the lost with the "wrong" motive. When the question arose of preaching the Gospel for the wrong reasons, Paul responded, "But what does it matter? The important thing is that in every way, whether from false motives or true, Christ is preached. And because of this I rejoice." (Phil. 1:18) I believe that any small seed of desire to share the Gospel or impact an unfamiliar people is living evidence that the Holy Spirit is drawing you into a bigger story.

Here are seven motives that will propel our lives toward a passionate pursuit of Jesus' primary purpose.

Obedience to the King

Some might readily admit, "I'm not there yet. Feeling the heart of God is foreign to me." That's okay. At times we need to launch our belief into motion and let our heart catch up!

Jesus instructed his disciples (which currently includes you and me), "...Go into all the world and preach the Good News to all creation." (Mark 16:15) This was not suggested but rather commanded. Jesus is the King and he deserves nothing less than our absolute, immediate, wholehearted, joyful obedience! Unfortunately, that is not always what he receives.

I recall my attitude as a teenager when my mother would tell me to clean my room. With a bit of a rebellious heart I would challenge the request with the question, "Why do I need to clean my room? I'm the only one in here." This would be met with the quick firm retort: "Because I said so!" That was never quite good enough as a teenager, but I would begrudgingly make a half-hearted effort. Looking back, myself a parent now, I recognize that my mom's reply was perfectly reasonable. Out of respect for my parents and the biblical command to honor them, I could have chosen to willingly clean my room simply because "she said so."

Do we, like rebellious teens, cop an attitude at Christ's command? "It's not my problem. I didn't make the mess. Why do you want me to go?" Father commands us to take the message of his love and the sacrifice of his Son to people who are desperate for hope and reconciliation to God. If Jesus is really the Lord of our life, isn't the simple truth that "he said so" enough for us? Or are we still acting like children making excuses or looking for a loophole? He is the King and beckons our obedience. In the words of the great missionary, Hudson Taylor, "The Great Commission is not an option to be considered; it is a command to be obeyed."

Despite my rebellious bent, sometimes when Mom would provide further explanation it would soften my grumbling heart. "Remember, we have guests visiting tonight and I want our house to look nice for them."

In truth, we shouldn't need another reason, but all throughout the Bible, Father has graciously provided abundant motives to inform and soften our grumbling hearts.

To Bring Joy to the Father's Heart

We don't need to serve God out of guilt or obligation. Father desires more than teeth-gritting compliance; he yearns to fill us with genuine passion—to fuel our hearts toward desiring to see all people reconciled to their rightful relationship with Father.

According to Webster's Dictionary, the word "passion" is defined as "the suffering of Jesus during the Crucifixion."[8] The action of Christ, so fueled by love for the lost, literally defines the word *passion*! Interestingly, *passion* can also be defined as martyrdom or a willingness to suffer for the cause of Christ. We can reflect the passion of Jesus by selflessly serving others. If you want to live a life of passion, allow Jesus' sacrificial love for the lost to be your heart motivation too.

Have you ever noticed the wording that the writer of Hebrews chose to describe the passion of Christ?

Let us fix our eyes on Jesus, the author and perfecter of our faith, who for the *joy* set before him endured the cross, scorning its shame, and sat down at the right hand of the throne of God. (Heb. 12:2)

Joy? Really? How is it possible that Jesus could approach his cross with joy? The answer is simple; he looked through the cross and he saw you! He understood what his suffering would accomplish and valued you and me so much that he approached the cross in joyful anticipation of redeeming us. Knowing the Father's heart, Jesus understood the joyous gift he was presenting to the Father...the restoration of the souls of his lost children.

> All this is from God, who reconciled us to himself through Christ and gave us the ministry of reconciliation: that God was reconciling the world to himself in Christ, not counting men's sins against them. And he has committed to us the message of reconciliation. (2 Cor. 5:18-19)

Father's longing heart is satisfied as his lost children return to him. He has given us, the redeemed, the privilege of sharing the message of reconciliation. Father is waiting for the day that this mission is fully accomplished and his children from every tribe and language are restored back to him.

Compassion for the Lost

> Jesus went through all the towns and villages, teaching in their synagogues, preaching the Good News of the kingdom and healing every disease and sickness. When he saw the crowds, he had compassion on them, because they were harassed and helpless, like sheep without a shepherd. (Matt. 9:35-36)

Clearly, Jesus' compassion for the hurting moved him. When I walked the streets of Mumbai on my first trip to India I had a similar sensation as I witnessed the masses in grave conditions of suffering.

The movie *Slum Dog Millionaire* portrays cruel slumlords purposefully crippling children to produce more effective beggars. Sadly, this is not an indulgent over-dramatization—I have encountered firsthand those similarly maimed, even by their own parents, then dispatched wounded to beg for their family. My heart was, and is, moved with compassion over their tragedies.

The devil proves an evil master and will ultimately inflict pain on his followers. In light of this, our compassion for the lost and hurting should move us to emulate Jesus' example.

> For [Jesus] has rescued us from the dominion of darkness and brought us into the kingdom of the Son he loves, in whom we have redemption, the forgiveness of sins. (Col. 1:13-14)

We have the privilege not only to understand compassion for the lost, but to partner with Jesus in rescuing them through the power of the Gospel.

Desire for Justice

It is not difficult to recognize prevalent injustices today. Issues such as human trafficking, abuse, AIDS, poverty and the killing of the unborn, raise up a righteous anger within us to defend the weak and defenseless. In particular, we have been called by God to defend the orphaned and widowed.[9]

While moved by a desire for justice, let us also consider the injustice of unequal access to the Gospel. While some dwell in places that seem to offer a lovely church on every street corner, others spend their entire lives devoid of Jesus' life-giving message. Nearly three billion people have not yet had the chance to hear the kingdom's Good News—not even once! Yet, we send only 2.4% of our missionaries and 1% of our mission offerings to reach those populations.[10] This is unjust!

How can we selfishly hoard the Gospel when so many have yet to hear it?

One cannot help but be impressed by the missionary journeys of the apostle Paul. What motivated him to travel so extensively to distribute the message of Jesus? In his letter to the Romans Paul gives us a glimpse of his passion to deliver the Gospel to those devoid of it. "It has always been my ambition to preach the Gospel where Christ was not known, so that I would not be building on someone else's foundation." (Rom. 15:20)

May our hearts be stirred with justice accordingly for those who have been abused by Satan's evils *and* for those who have been deprived of God's Word!

Desire to See the Return of the King

My heart stirs with a joyful anticipation when I consider the return of King Jesus. Imagine what it will be like for those alive on earth that will witness Jesus returning for his bride. The Bible provides insight into his second coming.

> According to the Lord's own word, we tell you that we who are still alive, who are left till the coming of the Lord, will certainly not precede those who have fallen asleep. For the Lord himself will come down from heaven, with a loud command, with the voice of the archangel and with the trumpet call of God, and the dead in Christ will rise first. After that, we who are still alive and are left will be caught up together with them in the clouds to meet the Lord in the air. And so we will be with the Lord forever. (1 Th. 4:15-17)

The book of Revelation describes the return of King Jesus as a mighty warrior!

> I saw heaven standing open and there before me was a white horse, whose rider is called Faithful and True. With justice he judges and makes war. His eyes are like blazing fire, and on his head are many crowns. He has a name written on him that no one knows but he himself. He is dressed in a robe dipped in blood, and his name is the Word of God. The armies of heaven were following him, riding on white horses and dressed in fine linen, white and clean… [16]On his robe and on his thigh he has this name written: KING OF KINGS AND LORD OF LORDS. (Rev. 19:11-14, 16)

I believe this time is drawing near; this generation could behold the return of the King! I hope to be a living witness to this spectacular sight. But I also understand that a condition for his return is the COMPLETION OF THE GREAT COMMISSION! While Jesus walked on earth he specified conditions for his return and his final mandate's fulfillment depends upon our obedience.

> And this Gospel of the kingdom will be preached in the *whole world* as a testimony to *all nations*, and *then* the end will come. (Matt. 24:14)

This succinct statement from Jesus provides clear instructions for all who long for his return. The original word for "nations" here is the Greek word *ethnos* and refers to what we commonly call "people groups." Jesus will not return until his mission is accomplished by taking the Gospel to every people group on earth. It is estimated that of the 7.6 billion souls in the world today, 3.15 billion reside in unreached people groups with little or no access to the Gospel of Jesus Christ. The Joshua Project has enumerated 17,015 unique people groups on earth with an estimated 7,080 of them considered entirely unreached.[11]

Regarding this, Oswald J. Smith once lamented, "We talk of the second coming; half the world has never heard of the first." Unfortunately, his statement is still true today.

Many have said, "No one knows the time of his return; Jesus could come back today!" While it is true that no one can know the specified day or hour of his return, we can be assured that Jesus is *not* returning today or tomorrow, because we have not yet met the conditions of his return as expressed by him and recorded in Matthew 24:14. The Gospel has not yet been preached to every people group (all nations, *ethnos*) in the world.

My heart, driven by a passion to see the return of the King, motivates me to mobilize workers to every people group that have yet to receive the Gospel. Like Simeon waited in faith for the coming of the Messiah and was rewarded with the privilege of meeting the Christ child,[12] let us not only wait but also work to meet the conditions for his return. Join with me in this endeavor and petition the King to send you to one of these most-literally lost tribes.

Zeal for the Worship of God

John Piper is passionate about God and his desire to see the nations worship him. In *Let the Nations be Glad*, he writes these impassioned words about the supremacy of worship, "Missions exists because worship does not. Worship is ultimate, not missions, because God is ultimate, not man. When this age is over, and countless millions of the redeemed fall on their faces before the throne of God, missions will be no more. It is a temporary necessity. But worship abides forever."[13]

David wrote songs to stir flames of worship for the living God. That zeal is expressed all throughout Psalms in words that divulge his desire for all peoples to exalt God.

May God be gracious to us and bless us and make his face shine upon us, that your ways may be known on earth, your salvation among all nations. May the peoples praise you, O God; may all the peoples praise you. May the nations be glad and sing for joy, for you rule the peoples justly and guide the nations of the earth. May the peoples praise you, O God; may all the peoples praise you. Then the land will yield its harvest, and God, our God, will bless us. God will bless us, and all the ends of the earth will fear him. (Ps. 67)

Notice importantly that the Great Commission is not a divine after-thought! This has always been God's expressed intention: for all peoples of earth to come into a reconciled relationship with God, and therefore worship the King! Our motivation for missions should embody this. We want God to receive the honor that he is due. Jesus has purchased souls from every tribe and tongue to worship him.

The revelation that the disciple John received highlights the worship that Jesus deserves for the sacrifice he made, not only for us, but also for those of every tribe on earth!

And they sang a new song: "You are worthy to take the scroll and to open its seals, because you were slain, and with your blood you purchased men for God *from every tribe and language and people and nation.*" (Rev. 5:9)

Two young Moravian missionaries, John Leonard Dober and David Nitschman, were willing to sell themselves into captivity for the oppor-tunity to reach slaves in the West Indies. As their ship departed from Copenhagen, Denmark in 1732, those on the pier could hear their dec-laration: "May the Lamb that was slain receive the reward of his suf-fering!" This became the battle cry of an entire missionary movement.[14] When we are filled with zeal for Jesus, no cost is too high to bring glory to his name.

Jesus proves worthy of our worship and our life-devotion! He poured out his life as a sacrifice. Our zeal for his honor desires worship in every language, from every people, in every nation. May Jesus enjoy the full reward for his suffering!

The Love of God

What was the Father's motivation to send his son on the greatest missionary journey of all time? Love!

For God so loved the world that he gave his one and only Son,
that whoever believes in him shall not perish but have eternal
life. (John 3:16)

Have you ever considered this epic mission from Jesus' perspective?
He left the comfort of heaven to go cross-cultural to reach a people who
would not accept him.[15] He was sent as a long-term field missionary
with full knowledge that this assignment would cost him his life, and
painfully so. Only one singular motive could precipitate such a sacrifice:
love.

Thus we serve a missionary God and are called to be like him, even in
this. We are called to *love* like him and we are called to *go* like him. After
Jesus' death and resurrection he appeared to his followers and charged
them: "...As the Father has sent me, I am sending you." (John 20:21b)

Do not miss the implications of his words. Jesus is dispatching us on
a mission in the exact way that the Father sent him on one! Going out
will cause discomfort and will require sacrifice. What motive will sustain
us through this undertaking? Love!

God's love for us and our responsive love for him will compel us
to live so that his mission is accomplished. We are each to be forever
branded by the love of God.

For Christ's love compels us, because we are convinced that
one died for all, and therefore all died. And he died for all, that
those who live should no longer live for themselves but for him
who died for them and was raised again. (2 Cor. 5:14-15)

The seven motives outlined here are not merely arguments to per-
suade you to pursue involvement in world missions. They are values that
address the core of our being. When we accept and hold to these seven
convictions, the master potter molds our lives into vessels that bring
glory to his name. We are commissioned to be part of his mission being
accomplished! We will never be satisfied by anything less.

*Jesus, forgive my lack of dedication to your Great Commission. I invite you
to instill these Biblical values into the core of my being, so that I will spend
my life for the sake of your glory. Let my own heart be fueled by your passion,
a passion for you, and a desire to reach the lost. Let your mission be accomplished in me. Amen.*

Accomplish It!

- Have you ever considered God as a father longing for his lost children? How might this understanding inform your life purpose?

- Of the seven heart motivations discussed in this chapter, which one do you most naturally connect with? Which one do you need to grow in the most?

- How might embracing these heart motives shape your future?

- Pray the "dangerous prayer" inviting Father to give you a revelation of his heart.

- Look for someone to share the Father's love with today. Consider practical ways and invite Holy Spirit's creativity as you do so.

Chapter 4

Top Priority

The Great Commission is not an option to be considered;
it is a command to be obeyed.
— Hudson Taylor

Eight years had passed since my life-impacting outreach to Mumbai, when finally I had the opportunity to return to the country that had left its unmistakable impression on me. By this time my wife, Kelly, and I had quit our jobs, sold our house and began to serve as missionaries with Youth With a Mission in Los Angeles. I had anticipated taking this second trip to India with my friend Dan, and wondered what new lessons God had prepared.

Dan and I traveled first to Kathmandu, Nepal and then crammed into a bus destined for a small, remote border town between Nepal and northeast India. The only hotel we could find was filthy. Rotting garbage heaped up against both walls framed a hallway path leading to our room. We pushed open the door to encounter a prison-like cell boxed in by four concrete walls, lit only by a bare bulb hanging from a wire delivering just enough electricity to flicker the area with an orange glow. Sheets on two single beds shadowed imprints of greasy brown stains, each in the shape of a person. Not wanting to entertain any more unpleasant thoughts about it than necessary, we quickly turned off the orange orb above us and fell into bed.[16]

At daybreak, our luggage in tow, we hiked across the border into India and scouted for a taxi to Siliguri to meet Dan's contact. We rounded a street corner to find a man positioned in front of a bus yelling, "Siliguri, Siliguri, fifty rupees." At just over a dollar to get to our destination, I thought things were starting to look up for us. Dan and I climbed on board and found two seats near the back, stowing our gear behind us. The bus lurched forward and before long we were bouncing along at a fast clip through the Indian countryside.

The wind ruffled my hair as I leaned out the bus window, soaking in the landscape as thoughts drifted back to my first India visit. As we passed irrigated fields of rice and the open countryside, I spoke to Jesus, "Lord, it's amazing to be back in India where you shaped my future. It was here that you showed me your heart for the lost and filled my life with purpose and direction. Lord, what do you want to teach me on this trip?"

Leaning out the window, I could see that our bus was fast approaching a village of thatched-roof, bamboo dwellings. I noticed a young man walking across the route ahead. Strangely, he did not continue crossing, but halted near the center of the road and turned to face our looming vehicle. I thought, *Why doesn't that boy get out of the way?* and grew more anxious as we neared. With only a bus length between us, my eyes met his desperate, hollow gaze. A moment later he flung his body into the front of our rushing bus.

I did not see the impact, but I heard and felt it: crushing bones and wheels lunging upward and over the young man's stricken body. I looked behind and saw his lifeless frame marking the road as our bus rolled on. My heart stopped beating, and I had to remind myself to breathe. *Oh God, why did I have to witness that? Out of all the buses, why did we ride this one? Why did I have to look into that boy's eyes?* The driver afforded no time to contemplate as he sped into the next city, steered directly to the police station, turned off the engine, and walked in.

An older gentleman leaned toward Dan and me and said, "I suggest that you leave as quickly as possible. You foreigners don't want to be around when the police start asking questions." We had not considered the risk, and though still stunned, we took the man's advice, exited the bus, hailed a taxi, and disappeared.

We made it to Siliguri, found our contact, and reached our guest-house: all a blur. I felt numb and knew I would not be alright until I could find a place to be alone with God. As I sat in bed that night in an unfamiliar place, the Lord began to bring revelation to my heart. I thought about how I had looked into that boy's desperate eyes, and I began to see him from the Father's perspective. I wrote in my journal:

> This was a child whom the Father loved deeply. And out of
> the billions of people on this planet, the Father mourns as if
> he has lost his only son. He has an infinite capacity to love.
> This young man was the precious work of his hands, a child for

whom Christ died. He was an unfulfilled longing in the Father's heart who desires all to come to the knowledge of Christ. If we could only see the reality of those dying daily, slipping into their eternal destiny in the absence of the Father who loves them and created them for intimate fellowship!

Jesus, I want to be propelled by a consuming passion of the Father's heart—seeing each and every person in this world as the precious work of your hands. May I spend my every day in a passionate pursuit of fulfilling the Father's will.

Father, bring some meaning to this senseless death by forever changing my perspective. I want to not only know your heart, but to be acutely aware of the urgency you have concerning each of your lost children. Keep me from the sin of apathy and complacency. I have seen too much to turn back. Help me move forward with fearless courage in obedience to your purpose for my life. Amen.[17]

Faces of the Lost

From that time onward, "the lost" has had a face: the countenance of a desperate young man with no hope, who never heard the Gospel. The face of a street child in Delhi peering through my taxi window, craving for anything to eat while I have the Bread of Life. And the face of a shopkeeper in Bangalore named Sarah, opening her heart in beautiful submission to the Savior when she first heard his story and prayed with me, entering into an everlasting love relationship with Father. Over seven billion people exist on this planet, each with a face. Each individually and intimately loved by the Father; each one in need of someone to show them the way to be reconciled to their Creator.

Freedom Found in Wholehearted Obedience

How do we make the Great Commission a priority in our lives?

I counsel you to begin with a simple prayer: "Jesus, I am willing to go anywhere, do anything, give everything. Whatever you ask of me, the answer is YES." Anything less than wholehearted obedience to the King is insanity!

There is a freedom that emerges when we surrender our lives to Jesus. We recognize that our lives are not our own, but have been purchased at a high price. Jesus takes not only control of us, but responsibility for us. I don't have to worry, because I'm in good hands as I trust that his plan is ultimately best! God does not call every person to go as frontline field missionaries, but he does call each one to be willing.

How could you ever be certain of your God-given calling without first approaching him with a willing heart? If you remain unwilling, it would be his act of mercy to withhold his calling rather than sentencing you to spend a life in conscious rebellion to the King's directive. You can trust that God's calling is constant with your unique design and will always prove the most rewarding.

What Moves You?

I think it is healthy to come clean about our priorities. Priorities are demonstrated not by our words but by our actions. We can evaluate priorities by how we spend our free time and money. Priorities are discerned in the content of our dreams and in what excites us when we talk with our friends. We all possess priorities, yet the question remains, is God's priority—to reach the world with the Gospel—evident among them?

What moves you? What do you consider important? Our core values compel us to action. The only way to effectively change our behavior is to modify our values.

We can believe something is true, yet our behavior remains unaffected. So ultimately, what moves you is what you value. Our love, our passion, our hunger defines our priorities. It's what makes us tick. It's our "why." The *reason* we do what we do.

If pursuing the things of God and fulfilling the Great Commission is not your priority, admit it. But please do not invent a theology to dismiss it. Rather, approach Abba Father in humility and invite him to change your priorities.

Priority Displayed in Giving

Christians, on average, give 2.5% of their income to charity. Clearly the Bible speaks of an up-front 10% tithe for believers, but the real amount speaks of actual priorities. Beginning in our second year of marriage, my wife Kelly and I prayerfully determined to increase our giving from 10% to at least 15% of our income. The bulk of our donations directly support missionaries working among unreached people groups. We want our personal giving to reflect our priority.

Let us suppose that Average Joe puts his monthly gift of $100 in the offering plate on Sunday, or 2.5% of the $4,000 he earned this month. Average First Church of America receives Joe's gift and designates $2.00 to missions. That's correct. On average, churches invest 2% of their income toward missions. Of the 2% thus given to foreign missions, 99% goes toward missionary efforts among those already reached or having access to the Gospel. Only 1% of those few missionary dollars actually goes toward sharing the Good News with those living within unreached people groups.[18] (See Appendix, Figure 3 for the distribution of our mission dollars.)

As a result, Joe's $4,000/mo. income contributed a meager two cents toward the completion of the Great Commission: just over a dime per year. Each of us should question whether we are demonstrating Christ's priorities through our giving.

I recently lost my dear friend, Tim, in a plane accident. Tim proved successful in business and his principles guided him and his wife to give back to God *90%* and live on the remaining 10% of their income! What if churches and ministries in which we participate, or even lead, were able to emulate Tim's example of giving toward the Great Commission? Tim and his wife prioritized the storing up of treasure in heaven; the bounty of which Tim is currently enjoying as a reward! We can be inspired by their faithful example.

I realize that money can be a touchy subject and I do not intend to offend. Perhaps, though, I prod because I have faced the painful truth that our meager world evangelism budget is not keeping pace against world population growth. This plight will only change when our priorities change.

Mission Drift

Is it fair to ask, "Have we lost our mission?" Remember from chapter 1, survey results showed that only half of our fellow Christ-followers acknowledge even *hearing of* the Great Commission, and only 17% can articulate its meaning.[19] This suggests that accomplishing Christ's command to go and make disciples is not our top priority.

In their award-winning book, *Mission Drift*, authors Greer and Horst offer the example of two great organizations that had their genesis in the streets of London in the mid-1800s. Both YMCA and InterVarsity were established to impact young lives with the saving message of Jesus Christ. If you are familiar with these two organizations you will recognize that one has held "mission true" while the other has become a sobering example of "mission drift."

The YMCA once stood for "Young Men's Christian Association" and spearheaded the Student Volunteer Movement, which became one of the most successful missionary recruiting agencies of all time. Christ resided at the core of everything they did. Now, it is known simply as the "Y" and primarily operates a chain of family fitness centers. It is a worthy endeavor, just not the purpose for which the association was founded.

> Everything flows from why. Not only does it motivate others to join you, it also guides what you do—and often more important—what you don't do. Having clarity of your purpose prevents the types of changes evidenced by the Y. "The single greatest reason for Mission Drift is the lack of a clear mission and vision," reflected David Wills, president of National Christian Foundation. "Crystal clear vision is the starting point for avoiding Mission Drift… if you don't know where you are going, any road will get you there."[20]

As we seek to align ourselves with the crystal clear vision established by Jesus himself, we would be wise to ask, "Have I individually, or we corporately, suffered from mission drift?"

Mission True

I have been encouraged lately by the emergence of "Great Commission churches." I'm impressed to see flags of the nations draping from their ceilings, often representing the countries of missionaries they actively support. Prayer guides and unreached people group profiles are readily available on back tables. Announcements include upcoming mission trips, not only for youth, but also for adults who utilize their areas of expertise in the field. Corporate times of prayer include intercession for missionaries and the people groups they are affecting. Individual worshipers emanate a general sense that their purpose aligns with the Great Commission, and that their participation is making a difference.

I've had some friends say "we attend a Great Commission church now and love it." I'm thrilled. But then I wonder, shouldn't *every* church be a

"Great Commission church?" Do we have the luxury of redefining our collective purpose when the King's mandate is painfully clear? The fact that we need a "Great Commission church" title distinction further indicates how woefully we have drifted from our God-given purpose. Remember, Jesus is inviting us into a purpose-filled, life-giving journey, both corporately and individually. Anything less will leave us dreadfully dull.

At this point, I can hear the clunking of rocks as fellow pastors and church members prepare for my public stoning! I hear the rebuttal. "We can't all be focused on missions. We have a responsibility to the lost in our community and to care for the needs of our people." I want to assure you of my wholehearted agreement. But our responsibility does not end there. Luke records one of the most poignant Great Commission scriptures in his book, "The Acts of The Apostles."

> But you will receive power when the Holy Spirit comes on you;
> and you will be my witnesses in Jerusalem, and in all Judea and
> Samaria, and to the ends of the earth." (Acts 1:8)

We often appropriately interpret "Jerusalem" as the city in which we live—as the disciples were in Jerusalem when Jesus made the statement. We can infer "Judea and Samaria" as our neighboring cities, states, provinces and countries, and "the ends of the earth" logically as everyone on the planet, including the unreached people groups still living today. (See Appendix, Figure 1 to see where those unreached people groups are concentrated.)

Yet notice that Jesus did not voice, "Jerusalem, *then* Judea, *then* the ends of the earth." Nor did he suggest, "Jerusalem *or* Judea, *or* the ends of the earth." Rather, Jesus provides his power for you to be a witness to your city *and* your state *and* your neighboring countries *and* the ends of the earth! Your desire to reach your city does not absolve you from your responsibility to the unreached, and my calling to share the Gospel with the unreached does not excuse me from being an effective witness to those in my local community. This is an important "both/and" proposition.

But we don't have to do it alone; we need each other. Missionaries and mission agencies depend upon the support and pastoral care of local churches. Likewise, churches benefit acutely from the experience and expertise of mission agencies that specialize in cross-cultural Great Commission work. I'll say it again, we do not have to go it alone. Reach out to a missionary friend and invite yourself along on his or her next outreach, or offer to visit a person out on the field. Your co-laborer in God's endeavor will be thrilled.

My goal in this chapter is not served by inducing guilt, but rather a healthy provoking. I want for us to honestly evaluate our priorities so we can realign them with God's priorities. We must reject any emerging feeling of condemnation—that leads us nowhere useful—and instead, bravely embrace the conviction of the Holy Spirit that precedes change.

Consider a constructive question: "What noticeable change would be evident in my life with my priorities aligned to the Great Commission? Where might I spend my time, money, and my vacation?"

In Bruce Wilkinson's book, *The Dream Giver*,[21] "Ordinary" is a nobody living in the Land of Familiar until the Dream Giver gives him a beautiful feather representing his Big Dream. Perhaps you are feeling ordinary and are currently comfortable with the familiar. Father has provided a big dream for your life. It's connected to his big dream of all the people groups gathered around his throne in joyful worship. When you take a step to accomplish his purposes, your life becomes anything but ordinary! But it will require taking a step beyond the familiar. Jesus has not only given you a big dream, but will empower you to achieve it!

Generate a plan to take steps consistent with your new priorities—your big dream. Perhaps jump into an online evangelism course, or study a foreign language. Sign up for a short-term mission among the unreached. Initiate a prayer group at your church. Support an indigenous missionary through a group such as Harvest Frontiers or The Timothy Initiative. As you respond, invite Holy Spirit to direct each step.[22]

Jesus, I'm ready. I want to make my life count for eternity. Jesus, I am willing to go anywhere, do anything, give everything. Whatever you ask of me, the answer is YES. I want my purpose and destiny to align with the Great Commission. As I consider the faces of the lost, show me how to make reaching them my top priority. Amen!

Accomplish It!

- What are some of your most important priorities at this stage of your life?

- Do you believe that the Great Commission should be the top priority for every believer? Why or why not?

- If the Great Commission is the top priority for Christians, would your life be a better example of "mission drift" or "mission true"?

- How can Great Commission activity be incorporated into priorities you are already working on?

- Giving can be an indicator of priorities. Consider giving directly to frontline work through www.harvestfrontiers.org or other frontier mission efforts and organizations.

Chapter 5

Mission Accomplished!

The Gospel is only good news if it gets there in time.
— Carl F. H. Henry

Hiking through the jungle of Equatorial Guinea with a team of Montana high school students brought exhilaration. "Who gets to do this?" their youth pastor, Debby, exclaimed as she stepped along just in front of me on a narrow winding trail. "I mean, I never dreamt I would experience Africa and share the Gospel alongside my youth group. How cool is that?" I shared likewise in Debby's enthusiasm. This excursion into "the bush" provided a welcomed change of pace from the past week's hectic schedule of daily ministry outreach to children in Bata, a major city. Each night we held evangelistic meetings in a different neighborhood, showing the *Jesus* film under the stars using a 16-millimeter projector and an oversized portable screen. The children would plant directly in front of the screen while men and women would stand for hours watching. You could hear gasps as they gazed upon the portrayal of Jesus healing the eyes of the blind or casting out a demon, and see tears as they saw the Christ beaten and killed. At each evening's conclusion we gave an invitation to follow Jesus as Savior and Lord, and I had never in my life seen so many responding to the Gospel! How fulfilling it was to see this evangelistic tool in action.

Only months prior to this, missionary leaders from Equatorial Guinea, Miguel and his wife Marlien, had visited the mission training center at which Kelly and I were serving. Sitting with us in our comfy "double wide" trailer living room, they began to pour out their hearts' request. "We have been hoping to use the *Jesus* film in our country," Marlien began. "We prayed for a projector and screen and the Lord has miraculously provided."

"Now all we need is the film on 16-millimeter reels," Miguel interjected. "Did you know that they speak Spanish in Equatorial Guinea? That's the language of the *Jesus* film we have been praying for—but it is very expensive to obtain."

Kelly and I exchanged knowing looks, and smiling, she cued me with a subtle nod. We had raised money years ago to acquire the 16-millimeter film in Spanish for trips we had led to Mexico with our previous youth groups. We had hoped to repurpose it in our current role, but it had yet to see much use. I momentarily excused myself to retrieve a large case from our storage shed. I returned, revealing the case and placed it on the coffee table in front of our new missionary friends. Bewildered, they stared up at us in astonishment.

Kelly answered the question before it was asked: "It's a complete *Jesus* film on 16-millimeter reels—in Spanish. It's now *yours* for your ministry! We pray that many will come to Christ through you guys."

Tears immediately poured as Marlien and Miguel hugged us and thanked us profusely. Miguel affirmed, "You cannot believe what an incredible answer to prayer you have just been to us. Thank you!" as he wrapped me in another big squeeze.

I never imagined that I would get to see this gifted *Jesus* film in action, but when our dear friend, Debby, called to tell me that she wanted to take her youth group on an overseas mission trip the next summer— and wanted me to lead them—I immediately sensed an opportunity the Lord was providing.

Now, mere miles away from the Equator, sweat flowed freely down our necks as we hiked through the humid foliage. We hoped by late afternoon to reach the church where we were scheduled for a program with African teens. When we happened upon a murky flowing river, Debby's boys, Nathan and Andrew, kicked off their shoes, stripped off their shirts and jumped in. Ryan, Biff and I followed right behind them. The girls didn't want to miss out so they also launched into the muddy water, wearing shorts and T-shirts. Pretty soon, most everyone enjoyed the river, splashing and laughing, grateful for the respite from the intense heat.

Libby, one of the first girls out of the water, noticed a slight trail of blood running down her leg. She thought she had perhaps scraped her leg on a rock, but soon began screaming upon discovering the source: a giant leech affixed to the back of her thigh. Abby and Jess scrambled quickly out of the water and discovered that they also were host to the slimy parasites. The guys then darted from the water finding ourselves covered with the bloodsuckers, since we had been submerged the longest. Quite the commotion ensued as we nervously plucked wiggling leeches off one another.

After recovering from the ordeal we continued down the thickly jungled path. Miguel began to walk near me on the trail, sharing stories that have ever since impacted my life.

"Marty, this hike with these teens reminds me of a recent outreach I led with African nationals from our last discipleship training school," he began, now walking side by side as the path broadened slightly. "I wanted to take them deep into the jungle, way farther than we are going today, because I had heard about a tribe rarely seen by outsiders who had never been exposed to the Gospel. I wasn't sure if we could find them or what their response would be if we did. We trekked through the jungle with machetes, blazing our own path and wading through rivers. When it seemed that there was no hope of finding this remote people group, we happened upon the tribe in the middle of the dense jungle.

"The chief, who was also a military leader, stepped forward and demanded, 'What do you want and why have you come?' He spoke the native dialect of Hausa that some of our students could understand and interpret.

"Chief, we wanted to meet you and your tribe," Miguel continued. "We have a very important message for you and your people."

After briefly consulting with his tribesmen he announced to Miguel and his team of young missionaries, "Very well, you are welcome to stay with us tonight and in the morning I will assemble the village to listen to the message you have brought us."

"We were grateful and excited for the open door that the Lord had just provided," Miguel shared. "In the morning, the chief assembled the entire village, just as he had promised. Then our team began to share the story of God. We started with the Creation account, then the sin of Adam and Eve, and then we explained that God had promised a Messiah who would restore man's relationship to God. We took turns explaining how Jesus came for that one purpose: To give his life as a sacrifice for sins so that we could be reconciled to the Father. Jesus had broken down the sin barrier that has kept us separated from God, and we need only to respond to his gracious gift by believing this message of Jesus and following him as the one true God."

The people of the village asked many questions and the team gave answers that were obviously inspired by the Spirit of God. Finally, the chief brought the meeting to a close. "Thank you for coming and sharing this important message with us." He announced. "I will meet with our elders tonight and in the morning we will give you our decision."

"And so they did," Miguel explained. "They met long into the early morning hours while our team prayed and interceded that the Holy Spirit would bring revelation to their hearts. The next morning they again assembled the village and my team and I were eager to hear what they had to say."

The chief stepped forward and spoke both to his people and Miguel's team. "The elders have come to a decision. We believe that the message these people have brought to us is true. We will follow Jesus Christ from this day forward!" There was no small commotion among the people and everyone seemed to be in enthusiastic agreement with the chief's announcement.

Miguel and his team decided to stay with the village and continue to disciple them. After weeks of instruction, the entire village assembled at the river to have a grand baptism ceremony in celebration of their newfound lives in Jesus.

Miguel paused for a while and we hiked before he shared the next part of the story, "Marty, after we had been with the village for some time, the chief approached me and I could tell something was troubling him. I asked if I could answer any of his questions. 'Something has been bothering me,' the chief began, reluctantly trying to find the right words, then blurted out, 'Is it true that Jesus was alive on this earth two thousand years ago?'

"'Yes, Chief, Jesus came to the world as one of us to show us the way to the Father.'

"'I understand *that*. But didn't you say that he told his followers to go into all the world and share this Good News with every tribe?'

"'Exactly, Chief, we call that the Great Commission.'"

Now the chief was visibly troubled, "But how is that possible? I don't understand. If Jesus told his disciples to share the Gospel with the whole world, how is it possible then that it has taken this long, TWO THOUSAND YEARS, for your people to bring this Good News to my people and my village?"

It was as if the chief carried the full weight of our historical disobedience to Christ's command on his own shoulders; "What about all our mothers and fathers and grandparents who have died without ever knowing about Jesus?"

At this point, Miguel stopped in the trail and looked straight into my eyes. "Marty, how would you have answered the chief?"

Shaken by his story, I responded the only way I could think of. "I would have said I was sorry," I offered. "I would have asked the chief for forgiveness. 'We, the followers of Jesus, have been disobedient to God's Great Commission command. Chief, on behalf of my people we are so sorry that it has taken this long for the message of Jesus to reach your village.'"

"That is exactly what I said to him," Miguel replied. And we continued onward in silence for a long time.[23]

> How, then, can they call on the one they have not believed in? And how can they believe in the one of whom they have not heard? And how can they hear without someone preaching to them? And how can they preach unless they are sent? As it is written, "How beautiful are the feet of those who bring Good News!" (Rom. 10:14-15)

The truth remains that the chief and his village were not able to believe in Jesus until Miguel and the beautiful young feet of his African team members arrived in person to tell them his story. There are countless tribes and villages the world over yet waiting to receive their Good News.

The Hard Truth About Completing the Task

I am compelled to state the obvious here, and it may be difficult to hear. In order to complete the Great Commission, we need to go share the Gospel where it has never been heard. The problem persists, though, that Christ's church has NOT prioritized sending workers to those without the Gospel. Currently, for every 31 missionaries we send out, only one will work among the unreached. (See Appendix, Figure 4.) The path of least resistance defaults our missionaries toward Gospel-reached areas. (See Appendix, Figure 2.) It is worthy and necessary work of follow-up and discipleship, but to complete the task we must equip a fresh army of missionaries who will take the Gospel into difficult—even hostile—places. The simple truth is the Great Commission will remain unaccomplished until the people of God obediently go to those devoid of the Gospel.

Well-intending believers have often asked me, "You're going to India again? Why travel across the world to tell someone about Jesus when there are people in our own country that don't know him?" I have to first discern that they are genuinely serious in their questioning. Then I don't know whether to laugh or cry. I must patiently remind myself that most believers do not understand the far-reaching ramifications of the Great Commission or what its accomplishment will require.

The Task is Achievable in this Generation

Christians, for our paradigm to shift, we need first to believe that completing the Great Commission is *achievable*! Have you ever simply asked yourself, *Can the Great Commission be completed?* Jesus would not have set us up to fail over an impossible task! For too long we have taken a view of Christ's mandate as the proverbial donkey chasing a carrot on a stick. The master, riding the cart in tow, dangles a carrot just in front of the donkey's nose. The donkey keeps pursuing but never attains its reward. After two thousand years, failing to recognize the progress made, we conclude the effort as futile. Ultimately, we kick the can down the road for a future generation to accomplish.

I can still hear the late Keith Green's voice as he pounded out chords at a concert I attended as a teenager. Green was a passionate follower of Jesus and one of the pioneers of contemporary Christian music. As Keith hammered the piano keys in introduction to one song, his distinct high-pitched voice cried out, "This generation of believers is responsible for this generation of souls." He challenged us to spend ourselves in fulfilling the Great Commission, "Instead of just sending your money—how about *going*?"

I had heard this impassioned charge at one of his final concerts prior to his untimely death in a plane accident. His anthem lives on through the countless youth he once inspired with a clarion call to missions.

We must approach the Great Commission with expectant faith— that the task is achievable, and that Jesus will work alongside us to accomplish this endeavor. HE is undeniably more vested in his interest in and commitment to the task than any one of us could ever be! Again, keep forefront in your mind: to accomplish the Great Commission, we must take the Gospel to those living without it.

I *do* believe that we will accomplish the Great Commission within my lifetime. This generation of believers will take the Gospel to every people group on the planet. The mission will be carried to completion by the faithful, such as you and I, willing to do whatever it takes to obey Jesus and to see for ourselves the King return for his bride!

Does my proclamation sound idealistic? Consider four reasons why you also can be optimistic about the completion of the Great Commission in your lifetime.

Never Has the Task Been So Clearly Defined

In recent history, three innovative pioneers brought clarity to the mission task: Donald McGavran (1897-1990), Cameron Townsend (1896-1982), and Ralph Winter (1924-2009).

> McGavran was one of the first to teach the concept of "people groups." Townsend applied that understanding to language translations and founded one of the world's largest missionary organizations, Wycliffe Bible Translators. Winter mainstreamed the focus on unreached people groups for the global church. Together, these three helped set the aims and strategy of the twentieth-century wave toward completing the Great Commission.[24]

Joshua Project and others have built on these forerunners' foundation by gathering information on unreached people groups (UPGs) so that mission organizations can focus their efforts on COMPLETING the Great Commission. As previously stated, of the 17,000 people groups on earth, 7,000 remain unreached with the Gospel. Not only do we know who these peoples are, we also know where they live. (See map, Appendix, Figure 1.) The vast majority of those unreached by the Gospel reside in the global region known as the "10/40 window"—a rectangular area from ten to forty degrees north of the equator, stretching from the west coast of Africa to the east coast of Japan.

Of the 7,000 unreached people groups, the 31 largest known as "Frontier Peoples," are less than 0.1% Christian in their populations and constitute a full 25% of persons worldwide with almost no access to the Gospel. If you are wondering where to get started, visit www.go31.org and then ask Jesus how you can engage one of these groups through prayer, giving or going.

Further definition of the mission at hand is credited to Paul Eshleman, founder of "Finishing the Task," who is currently shining a spotlight on remaining Unengaged Unreached People Groups (UUPGs). These are unreached people groups, typically small in population, without a single missionary living among them. Like the chief and his tribe in Equatorial

Guinea before Miguel and his team encountered him, these UUPGs have not yet been engaged with the Gospel—not even once. Through focused missionary efforts, the UUPG number has now been whittled down to less than one thousand.

The unfinished task is clearly defined, and now within reach. It's time for every member of the body of Christ to engage in the effort with this information.

Never Have We Seen Such Coordinated Efforts by the Body of Christ

My friend, Colin Millar, was a businessman in South Africa when the Lord clearly spoke to his heart, "Your hose and gasket business is over. I'm calling you to ignite prayer for the nations and I will provide for all your needs." Colin obeyed that word from God and founded "Igniting Prayer Action" to unite the body of Christ in passionate prayer until God's kingdom comes.

For Colin, prayer became the key to building collaborative, Great Commission-accomplishing relationships across denominational lines. He told me, "God is building Jesus joy-filled friendships, weaving us into an ever-clearer tapestry of prayer united for church planting movements." These knitted relationships established The Global Alliance for Church Multiplication (GACX) in 2011; a global network of more than 75 kingdom-building partners.

GACX declares some gutsy God-sized goals! They share a common vision to plant five *million* healthy, sustainable, reproducing churches—a church for every thousand-person community on earth! They are not alone in their aggressive collaborative goal-setting. "24:14," a network focused on multiplying church planting movements, is working to ignite faith movements within every unreached people group by 2025![25]

Other rapidly expanding networks mirror such audacious goals, working together to finish the task outright in the near future. Are these movements driven by impractical dreamers, or propelled by those simply listening to the Holy Spirit communicating the heart of God?

I believe that now is the time to come together and that Jesus invites us to link arms with fellow brothers and sisters in Christ, regardless of denominational backgrounds. We must become less concerned with promoting our brand of Christianity and more focused on announcing the Good News of Jesus to every corner of the planet—until no place remains where his name is unknown!

Never Have We Seen Such a Push to End Bible Poverty

We cannot underestimate the significance of the Word of God in the task of completing the Great Commission. Yet many people groups remain without any access to Holy Scripture. This is termed, "Bible poverty."

Cameron Townsend founded Wycliffe Bible Translators with the goal of making the Bible accessible in the heart-language of every tribe on earth. After 75 years of labor, their enormous task still seemed a long way off. In the year 2000, Wycliffe leaders evaluated their progress and determined that, at their current rate, it would require another 150 years before a Bible translation could be initiated in every remaining language. Wycliffe team member, Bob Creson stated, "As emerging local partners and churches exploded, and technology radically cut the time needed to complete a translation, they knew they could do better. Wycliffe trusted God's heart for the people of the earth… and set an audacious, aggressive, seemingly impossible goal of having a Bible translation project underway in every language by the year 2025."[26]

Wycliffe's modernized goal is now called "Vision 2025." About one-third of the 7,000 spoken languages worldwide have adequate *access* to Scripture and another 2,200 languages have translation projects currently in progress. Yet there remain 1,600 communities afforded no access to the Bible in their heart-language. The faithful workers at Wycliffe believe that with the help of the Holy Spirit, they can launch the remaining translation projects by the year 2025!

Ending Bible poverty not only requires translation, but also distribution. We at YWAM Idaho recently sent a "backpackers' outreach" to distribute Bibles with the help of my "Nepali son" David. He navigated our team into a remote region of Nepal, each member's pack bulging with Bibles, and their legs buckling from hours of strenuous hiking. After a twelve-hour load-bearing journey, and still two hours from their final destination, David stopped and laughed as he exclaimed, "This is where the government census ends; they don't even bother counting people beyond this point." Yet the lives beyond census lines matter to God, and he wants them to know his Word.

Loren Cunningham, founder of Youth With A Mission, in his recent book, *We Can End Bible Poverty Now*, poses the question, "Is it possible to end Bible poverty all over the world?"

It is if we all do our part. No one organization or movement has the resources to finish Bible translation, production, and distribution. Our resources are like the five small barley loaves and two fishes. We must see what is already in our hands. Everyone has something. We need to pray, give financially, and go—whether next door or to the remotest island, jungles, and mountain villages in the world.[27]

Each of us can contribute something toward ending Bible poverty around the world. Offer your own loaves and fishes and watch Jesus bless and multiply your effort until the Word of God is available to all.

Never Have We Seen Such Prayer Concentrated on Finishing the Task

From Pentecost and the Apostle Paul, right down through the centuries to the present day, the story of missions has been the story of answered prayer. Every fresh outbreak of missionary energy has been the result of believing prayer. Every new missionary undertaking that has been owned and blessed of God has been the germinating of seed planted by the divine spirit in the hearts of praying saints.[28]

I recently interviewed my friend, Liz Adleta, a key global prayer strategist, inviting her to share insights on prayer and missions.

Marty: How have coordinated global prayer movements developed and how do they contribute to finishing the task for Jesus?

Liz: Certainly much of the exciting developments in concerted prayer for unreached peoples had their roots in the AD2000 and Beyond Movement during the 1990s which led to prayer teams being onsite and praying with insight among unreached people groups, especially those within the 10/40 Window. Next we saw God use the annual Global Day of Prayer to create prayer networks in every nation and region throughout the world. Focused prayer made way for unprecedented church planting movements in which rapid growth and multiplication can only be attributed to a work of God. Research has shown that only extraordinary prayer can bring this type of extraordinary fruitfulness.

Marty: Liz, how do you see prayer movements and mission movements uniting?

Liz: The Moravian missionaries were birthed out of a hundred-year nonstop 24/7 prayer meeting. Today, we see major prayer movements and mission movements coming together in active collaboration. Houses of Prayer, Boiler Rooms, and Strategic Prayer groups are building a foundation of intercession and worship focused on finishing the Great Commission.

Marty: What gives you hope of seeing God's mission accomplished?

Liz: One of the most dramatic indicators is the readiness of key leaders to focus on Jesus and establishing *his* kingdom. Instead of trying to make a name for ourselves, we are passionate about seeing his glory fill all the earth. As God continues to move our hearts in this way, it is easily to imagine every tongue, tribe, and nation hearing the Gospel very soon!

Friends, as you continue to read the next section of this book, you will discover a map unfolding before you. It reveals the path you were destined to travel and will lead you toward life's greatest gratification: joining the quest to complete the mission Jesus initiated over two thousand years ago. That mission is reconciling people from every tribe and language to a relationship with Father God. Jesus completed his work on the cross. He then authorized us to go and share this message with the whole world until we see his mission accomplished!

Jesus, I want to be a part of what you are doing in the earth today that will bring a culmination to the task you have for us. Even if I cannot see the whole map that you have laid out for me, I ask you to show me the next step. I desire to follow you, but need faith and boldness. Make me aware of your constant presence in this journey of obedience. Please direct my course to follow the life-giving destiny you desire for me. Amen.

Accomplish It!

- Does it come as a surprise that for every single missionary sent to work among the unreached, thirty are sent to Gospel reached areas? What can be done to shift the tide toward mission completion allocation?

- What difference might it make if we approached the Great Commission as an achievable task?

- Do you think engaging all the remaining unreached people groups can be accomplished in *your* lifetime?

- This chapter outlined four major factors indicating that completing the Great Commission is within reach. Which one most encourages and inspires you? Which of the four might you engage in directly?

- Feed your passion for missions by acquiring a book from the "Christian Heroes Then and Now" series: www.ywampublishing.com.

Part 2: Unlock the Purpose of Your Design

As you love God and serve Him, you will undoubtedly experience the greatest adventure life has to offer.

— Dr. Bill Bright

Chapter 6

Discovering Your Fit in the Great Commission

The real secret of an unsatisfied life lies too often in an unsurrendered will.
— Hudson Taylor

Chris stood out as an untamed skater kid with a blue mohawk and tattered black clothes—like he might bring trouble. He arrived with his youth group from a Korean church in the Seattle area. They attended the summer Mission Adventures program that Kelly and I led, which consisted of four days of training and six days of outreach. The team ate up the experience, and as I grew to know Chris I found him to be a regular teen with crazy hair, just trying to find his fit in life.

The following September I had the opportunity to visit Chris' church and speak to the youth group. Immediately upon arriving, Chris approached me with wild excitement. "Marty, I want to tell you that the Mission Adventures program last summer was crazy awesome, but nothing compared to what happened after I got home. Can I tell you about a vision that Jesus gave me?"

Clearly, he had my attention, "Of course, I'd love to hear about it."

"Well it came as a dream, only different, it was as if it actually happened. I was walking down the street carrying my skateboard with my gang when Jesus pulled up alongside us in his white pickup truck." At this point I wanted to interject the obvious question, but Chris continued on, considering it totally normal that Jesus would be driving a white pickup, so I refrained from interrupting.

"Jesus rolled down his window, looked in my eyes and said, 'Chris, do you want to come with me?' 'Sure, why not?' I replied, and threw my skateboard in the bed of his truck and away we went. He took a turn that led to a mountain near my city and the truck began to climb the switchbacks to the top. When we arrived at the summit, Jesus and I jumped out of the truck and made our way over to the observation deck. I was shocked by what I saw. My city below was completely flooded, and people were drowning, crying out for help. I was horrified. 'Jesus, those people are dying! Why don't you go down there and help them?' I said."

"'Chris, that's why I brought you up here to show you this,' he said to me. 'I want you to go down there and help them.' Then I woke up, but I had this strange sensation that the event was actually *real*!"

"Chris, do you understand what your vision means?" I asked.

"I think it means that I have a call on my life," he replied through a sidewinder smile.

"I agree. It sounds to me like an evangelistic call. Jesus wants you to save those who are lost and dying by sharing the Gospel with them." I gave Chris a copy of Loren Cunningham's book, *Is That Really You, God?* "In this book you're going to read about a young man who had a different kind of vision concerning water. Young Loren saw waves of young people crashing onto every continent, bringing the Good News of Jesus wherever they went. That vision was the inspiration for Youth With A Mission and its waves are now reaching every country on earth. I think Jesus has shown you this vision to reveal the purpose he designed you for."

I was filled with excitement when Chris's youth group signed up for another outreach the following summer. I greeted each student as they stepped off the bus, but was visibly disappointed when I discovered Chris was not among them. His brother, Glenn, recognized my concern, "Hey Marty, are you looking for Chris? He couldn't make it this year, but he told me to say 'Hi' to you." Glen continued, "That crazy brother of mine, I bet he was in the principal's office as much as he was in class this past year!" Interpreting the shock on my face, Glen was quick to add, "Oh, no, it's not what you think: Chris just won't stop sharing about Jesus at school. He's still the same wild kid, but one-by-one he's leading his skater friends to Jesus!"

I realized that Chris was indeed finding his fit according to the unique design Father had created him for. That's the challenge for each one of us, really, to find our fit; to discover our own unique role in completing the Great Commission (even if gets us into a little hot water). That is this chapter's objective, but first let's recap what we have learned so far.

Quick Review

Jesus directed his followers with the Great Commission, the joyful though difficult task of sharing the Good News of salvation and making disciples among all people groups (*ethnos*) on earth.

The Great Commission is not an optional activity, but the primary purpose of every Christian. Although all are not called as long-term field missionaries among the unreached, each of us is called to be willing to go. Whether or not we are among those that go, fulfilling Christ's mandate remains our top priority and each individual has a role to play in this.

We only find ultimate fulfillment by aligning our lives with God's primary purpose. We know that God is good and trustworthy; his plans are always best for our lives.

To accomplish the Great Commission, we must go to places void of the Gospel. The lost await this Good News as God also awaits and anticipates that we deliver it.

So then, how can we discern God's plan? How are we to discover our unique roles in the Great Commission?

Follow the Buck

I had designated three days to fast—to deprive myself of food and drink, only water—for the purpose of praying, and seeking God's direction for specific decisions. On the third day I planned to spend every minute with Jesus. I loaded my daypack with water bottles, carefully tucked in my Bible and journal, and hiked into the San Gabriel Mountains north of Los Angeles. I followed a footpath to a saddle between a slight knoll and a sizable peak.

I paused to catch my breath and decide whether to continue to the right or left. I wouldn't normally pray over such a minor decision but I asked, "Jesus, what direction do you want me to go?" I felt an immediate impression. The response struck me as odd: *Follow the buck.*

As an experienced hunter from Idaho, I recognized *buck* as a male deer with antlers, but I had never encountered one throughout my several years exploring these southern California hills. I had occasionally spotted a doe, but never one buck. "Okay...Jesus...you want me to follow the buck...." Silence. The memorized words from Isaiah 30:21 flashed into my mind: *Whether you turn to the right or to the left, your ears will hear a voice behind you, saying, "This is the way; walk in it."* Still though, no buck.

I reasoned that Jesus might simply want me to find the kind of place where I think a buck would go, which would mean turning left, to the higher peak including trees and better cover. Thus I took my first step in that direction. Before I could take another, a loud crashing startled me, sounding from some bushes just below. A magnificent buck, displaying four antler points on each side, emerged from the thicket. He bounded to the smaller knoll to my right, paused momentarily upon it, glanced over his shoulder as if to inform me, *This way, silly*, then disappeared as quickly as he arrived, into the brush below.

With a newfound keen sense of discernment, I started back to my right and set up my portable Bible study on the gentle knoll overlooking the city. During my time with Jesus I felt prompted to inquire, "What was all that buck business about, Lord? That was kind of a dramatic response to such an insignificant question." I wondered if perhaps my attempt at climbing the mountain peak in my depleted state of fasting might have had a disastrous end. As I waited and listened I perceived his still, quiet voice: *Marty, I want to give you my guidance in both small matters and big life decisions. You just have to stop and ask for direction.*

How often have we missed God's direction simply by failing to stop and ask for it? For months following this, I placed a small-size stickie note on the upper corner of my laptop where I wrote, "Pray about everything." Though simple, it typically proves true that to hear God's voice we must be listening—and listening usually presumes that we have asked! The first step toward finding your destiny is not a step at all, but rather time for pause and prayer.

Barges and Battleships

The summer after my first year of college I experienced a terrible motorcycle accident, a story chronicled in *Epic Faith*. I suffered a gash in my head and compressed vertebrae in my lower back but considered myself fortunate to still be alive. The significance of the ordeal rested in an important decision I made as I recovered from the incident lying in a hospital bed. I declared to Jesus that I wanted him to take charge of my life. "Jesus, I know that as long as I'm in control, I'm going to make a mess of things. I want to follow you as the Lord of my life. I give you complete control."

Years later, I marvel how that one decision ultimately shaped my life, and I am profoundly grateful for the course he has chosen for me as a result. Once, while pondering the outcome of that decision, an illustration invaded my thoughts: two very different sea vessels, a barge, and a battleship. The barge appeared quite boring, stacked simply with big shipping containers atop one another and a few workers sitting idly by. The battleship, on the other hand, stood impressively, with each person on board clad neatly in uniform and busied with important assigned duties. The battleship emanated purpose, and everyone on board participated in it. I felt a little nudge from the Lord, "On which ship would you rather be?"

"That's easy, I'll take the battleship over the barge any day!"

It occurred to me that this represented two contrasting perspectives in Christianity. Some Christians merely want to know that at their life's end they will get entry to heaven. In the meantime, they accept a long, boring trip, but the barge will eventually haul them there. Their one expectation from their limited faith perspective is that they will get to go to heaven after they die.

Other Christians regard themselves involved in a great conflict— that of combat for the rescue of lost souls. These have signed on actively aboard the battleship, considering the mission loaded with purpose and their individual role uniquely significant. They acknowledge only one requirement to enlist: absolute commitment to the one Commander and Chief. Aboard the battleship, disobedience to Jesus is not an option.

Once, while sharing this illustration with a class of high school students to challenge them to live with purpose for the cause of Christ, one spirited young man raised his hand and offered a third vessel option: "How do I sign up for the pleasure cruise?" (I suspect that many adults default to this option as well but practice restraint in not asking such a question.) I laughed out loud until I soon came to the realization that this teen's remark was intended as a serious suggestion.

I realized that there is an undeniable band of professing Christians in the same boat (pardon the pun) as this young man. They desire entertainment and amusement, comfort and indulgence. Like the passengers aboard the spaceship *Axiom* in the sci-fi animation *WALL-E*, they become so spiritually fat they can hardly move. For this faction, the entire Christian experience is summed up in *What can God do for me?*

From where did such ideology come? Certainly not from Jesus, who described his ambition in this way: "For even the Son of Man did not come to be served, but to serve, and to give his life as a ransom for many." (Mark 10:45) But whether you find yourself inclined toward barging or cruising through life, I invite you to surrender your life to the Commander and discover the battle-ready, life-giving purpose of your commission.

A Destiny Within

The spring semester of college following that summer motorcycle accident, my roommate, Doyle, busied himself in preparation for a summer cycling trip across Europe with his brothers. I struggled to hide my envy as I watched my chum open mail-ordered packages and assemble his gear. The giant slender box containing the Motobecane touring bicycle arrived first, succeeded by other parcels supplying cycling gloves, jerseys, panniers and a bike helmet. I envisioned places Doyle and his brothers would experience pedaling their way across Switzerland, Germany and France. Simmering in jealousy, I wondered if ever in my lifetime I would venture overseas. I had been taken to Canada and Mexico on family vacations but had yet to board my first airplane. I honestly couldn't think of any reason why I might encounter the opportunity to travel abroad. Would I ever make an impact beyond the little town of Winfield, Kansas where I grew up? The nagging question lingered, "What if I were created for something more?"

Today, many years later, I can reflect on that temporary sense of jealousy and realize that God used it to plant a deep longing in me to participate in a plot much bigger than my life up to that point. Ironically, I have since toured around the world numerous times—to India in particular, at least fifty times—propelled by his passion in my heart to see the nations worship Jesus.

Likewise, God has deposited a destiny within you.

For we are God's workmanship, created in Christ Jesus to
do good works, which God prepared in advance for us to do.
(Eph. 2:10)

This verse is a firm guarantee of the destiny God has for each one of us. A "destiny" is a predetermined ordering of events. God has a great plan for us and has deposited within each of us a wealth of his brilliance. Our destiny lies in discovering those gifts and then using them for his glory.

My wife, Kelly, enjoys posing the question, "What did you find your-self playing and enjoying when you were free and uninhibited as a child?" She often asks it when counseling young people questioning what they should do with their life. Consider the question yourself. There's a good chance that your childlike activities and roleplaying scenarios hold clues to your God-given destiny within.

So what are the keys to discovering how God has designed you, and how does that harmonize with his eternal purposes?

Keys to Your Future

Have you ever had the task of trying to unlock a door with an unfamiliar set of keys? You might simply work through the dangling hardware, trying each in succession, which can be frustrating and unnec-essarily laborious. On closer inspection, rather, you might omit those keys that obviously wouldn't fit. An assortment of padlock keys and that one that opens the paper towel dispenser definitely won't help. Next you might identify and skip all the car keys. Examining the remaining door keys, you could at last narrow the search by noting the groove patterns until you diagnose the best few candidates that might unlock the door. Now you can swiftly find and employ the right one.

As a young person, the door to your future may seem impossible to unlock. You may need to collect some experiences to find the right fit. And some things, you will intuitively discover, simply do not suit you.

I knew always that I was not cut out to be an accountant. I hated math and could not sit still for a reasonable length of time. Yet no busi-ness, church or mission organization could function without financial expertise present. I'm thankful that God has called others who are per-fectly suited for that role.

What motivates you? What energizes your heartbeat? What natural gifts and abilities do you possess? Apply those capabilities, and you will eventually unlock doors of gratifying purpose.

Those more mature in life, with a wealth of experiences, have oppor-tunity to refine their search for purpose. With some discerning times of reflection, one can evaluate what has proven most fulfilling among vari-ous areas of contribution. I have encountered many second-career adults who have discovered that the very skills they cultivated throughout their younger years can also be wielded as indispensable tools for the Great Commission.[29]

Your Greatest Gift is You

Recognize that you can make a difference right now. You may currently be unaware of the opportunities for impact within your present sphere of influence, but be assured: the greatest gift you can bring to the table is *you*!

> In 1975 God spoke to Loren Cunningham, Bill Bright, and several other Christian leaders that there are seven spheres of life which influence the values and beliefs of any society: education, church, family, government, business and technology, the performing arts and the media.
>
> Modern society is complex. In the midst of this complexity, God has promised that he has prepared good works for *you* (Eph. 2:10). You have a contribution to make. In this larger context of advancing God's kingdom on earth, what are the good works that he has prepared for *you specifically*? Uncertainty can keep us from stepping out and stepping up to the role of influence and service God has designed for us.[30]

As we unpack the list of seven spheres, the opportunities prove limitless. You can begin making an impact for God right now! Are you a student? A teacher? Part of a home school co-op? Do you belong to a church? A family? Have interest in politics or government? Do you own or serve a business? Do you interact with technology? Perform in or enjoy the arts? Are you involved with media? Every "yes" presents opportunities to advance God's kingdom.

You already interact in places of influence. You already possess unique giftings and abilities. Your destiny is inseparably connected to whom God has uniquely created you to be. *You* are the greatest gift you can bring to help fulfill the Great Commission! The time has come to put YOU into action.

A Ship and its Rudder

I want to assure you that God has devised plans for your life that will exceed your expectations!

> God can do anything, you know—far more than you could ever imagine or guess or request in your wildest dreams! He does it not by pushing us around but by working within us, his Spirit deeply and gently within us. (Eph. 3:20-21 MSG)

"For I know the plans I have for you," declares the LORD, "plans to prosper you and not to harm you, plans to give you hope and a future. Then you will call upon me and come and pray to me, and I will listen to you. You will seek me and find me when you seek me with all your heart." (Jer. 29:11-13)

Step forward in faith toward seizing the calling for which you were created. The Lord will be with you and will surely complete you for the pursuits you begin for his glory!

Did you notice that each chapter in this section of the book begins with a verb; a word spurring you to action? Discovering your role in the Great Commission begins by providing momentum towards your goal, while letting God steer. "In his heart a man plans his course, but the LORD determines his steps." (Prov. 16:9)

A vessel requires motion for the rudder to function.

Or take ships as an example. Although they are so large and are driven by strong winds, they are steered by a very small rudder wherever the pilot wants to go. (Jam. 3:4)

Jesus intends to pilot you into the good plan he has charted for you. Father desires that you participate in this discovery finding your purpose connected with his. He has created you to embark on a great adventure with him. Every epic journey begins with a first step.

Jesus, show me the next step you have for me in discovering my destiny. I want to enlist for the battleship and fulfill every purpose you have for my life. I believe that I was created for a purpose that is greater than myself. I want to be used by you to advance your kingdom and bring glory to your name. I invite you to set my vessel in motion. Amen.

Accomplish It!

- How can you discern God's plan and discover the unique roles he has prepared for you in the Great Commission?

- In what ways do you personally relate to the illustration of barges, battleships and pleasure cruisers? What is required to enlist for service on the battleship? Have you done so?

- The greatest gift you bring to Jesus is you! What talents and abilities has God deposited in you that you can give back to him for mission accomplishment?

- What small step could you take today to get your ship in motion?

- If you are a young person, consider connecting with www.missionadventures.net, if you are an adult consider engaging www.missionbuilders.org.

Chapter 7

Pray: Unleash Mountain-Moving Power

To be a Christian without prayer is no more possible
than to be alive without breathing.
— Martin Luther

I had never presented the Gospel on the street, but my heart came alive at one of the busiest intersections in Paris, proclaiming the Good News of Jesus. I was 25 years old and my around-the-world evangelism team had just finished a redemption-themed drama set to music. A huge crowd had gathered on the corner, impeding normal foot traffic. Immediately after the drama, a French evangelist jumped up and started preaching. Though I couldn't understand what he was saying, his passion for the message of the cross pierced through the chatter. He held the crowd's attention with his strong voice and grand sweeping gestures. Our team squatted on the sidewalk near the preacher while most bystanders stood scattered about to listen. With the French orator still getting warmed up, I overheard my friend Kip begin to pray for a taxi driver he had noticed who was stopped at the intersection, one elbow hanging out a rolled-down window. Kip's prayer and intensity impressed me as he squeezed out each request, "Jesus, get that guy right there in his taxi cab. I pray that every word this preacher speaks right now would pierce his heart. Don't let him go, God. Make him stay right there in his taxi until he has heard this entire Gospel message."

Just as I started to think that perhaps Kip was going a little overboard with his intercession, an amazing thing happened. The traffic light turned green and the taxi remained stationary. Drivers behind him honked repeatedly, then swerved around him offering obscene gestures, but the taxi driver didn't budge. He seemed instead transfixed by the preacher, and I suspected that Kip's prayer had a lot to do with it.

"That's right, God, you've got his attention now!" Kip prayerfully continued, his eyes like laser beams on the unsuspecting soul.

At that moment my attention shifted to what appeared to be a sizable woman sporting a five-o'clock shadow, who had recently joined the crowd of spectators. Though wearing a long floral-print dress and a blonde wig, it was obvious to me that this was no woman. Inspired by Kip's prayer seizure, I began to earnestly pray for the gender-confused individual before me. "Jesus, I see this person standing over there and I pray that he would be captured by your love. Reveal to his heart that he was created to be a son of God. Jesus, as he listens to the words of the Gospel, restore this man to a right relationship with the Father." Even as I prayed, I felt the Lord softening my own heart and creating tenderness within me for this man I had never met.

I did not understand French, but it was obvious that the evangelist was bringing his message to a conclusion as he began challenging his listeners to turn their hearts over to Jesus. That is when I witnessed an unexpected miracle. The taxi driver promptly shifted his vehicle into park without cutting off the engine, sprang out of his cab and knelt on the sidewalk. Moments later he was joined by a man in a floral dress. As the two prayed with the evangelist to receive the love and forgiveness available through Jesus, Kip and I instinctively relocated to kneel beside them, placing our hands on their shoulders and blessing them as they uttered the most important commitment of their lives.

Partner with Jesus in Prayer

Years later, I shared the story above with my youth group prior to leading them on a mission trip to Mexico. "I'm going to be preaching the best I know how, but I want you guys to be praying just like Kip and I did on that street in Paris. Just pick one person out of the crowd and start praying earnestly for them."

We set up our puppet stage in a crowded park buried within the bustling city of Mexicali, Mexico. Our puppet play was set to a Spanish recording and *niños* rushed in from all directions, dragging their parents along with them. Next we performed two dramas set to music, which further drew in a cautiously interested teenage crowd. Then my opportunity to preach arrived, but because of a communication breakdown earlier in the day, we lacked a translator for this particular venue of evangelism. I queried awkwardly over the PA system, "Does anyone here speak English who can translate for me?" One man reluctantly weaved his way forward, so I handed him the second mic connected to our portable sound system and began to preach. While struggling to get into a rhythm with my new acquaintance-turned-translator, I noticed a rogue gang of teens join the crowd while their obvious ringleader hung back, leaning against a nearby tree, arms pressed across his chest.

It wasn't long into my message when we got on a roll as my excitement for the Good News grew contagious, even to my translator. Things continued well, as far as I could tell, until I offered an invitation to come forward and receive Jesus Christ as Savior and Lord. Unmoving, blank stares were the only reply. My heart had grown so expectant that some were destined for salvation that day, so I again summarized the Gospel and attempted another appeal. I felt stirred so as to boldly announce, "There is someone here that needs to receive Jesus as Savior today. Come forward now and receive new life through Christ. Who is it that needs salvation?"

To my shock, the distant young man propped against the tree shot up a hand and yelled, "Mi Señor!" He labored his way to the front and knelt in the center of the plaza. He was soon joined by a dozen of his rogue counterparts. Then my makeshift translator set down his mic and knelt on the pavement beside the teens! As this contrite group poured out their hearts to God in Spanish, my entire youth group surrounded them in prayer just as Kip and I had done years before. One could tangibly feel the presence of God in that hallowed plaza. What an indescribable atmosphere!

Later, we disassembled the puppet stage and started hauling equipment back to the van. One of my students, Jason, hurried to catch up to me as I lumbered with a heavy speaker. "So, was that pretty much what you expected, Marty?" Jason asked excitedly.

My eyes were still reddened with emotion, "Jason, what happened in this park today went *way beyond* my expectations."

"Well, you know that guy who stepped forward when it seemed like no one was going to respond and then that one young man leaning against the tree did?" Jason could hardly contain his excitement as he spoke.

"Of course I know who you're talking about," I smiled. "His step of obedience broke the barrier so that others would come forward."

"I just wanted to tell you…" Jason blurted, "That was the guy I was praying for!"

I became so proud of him in that moment. "Jason, you took the opportunity to partner with Jesus in prayer. Your faith made the difference and you got to see God work in that young man's heart today!"

> Jesus said, "I tell you the truth, if you have faith as small as a mustard seed, you can say to this mountain, 'Move from here to there' and it will move. Nothing will be impossible for you.'" (Matt. 17:20)

When we pray, things happen! You can even move hearts with prayer.

All Nations Will Be Blessed Through You

Back when God spoke to Kelly and me saying, "Quit your jobs, sell your house and go to a place I will show you," he confirmed that word through Genesis 12:1-3:

> The LORD had said to Abram, "Leave your country, your people and your father's household and go to the land I will show you. I will make you into a great nation and I will bless you; I will make your name great, and you will be a blessing. I will bless those who bless you, and whoever curses you I will curse; and all peoples on earth will be blessed through you."

Based on this scripture we had taken a daunting step of faith, quitting our jobs, selling our house, and enrolling in a Discipleship Training School. We were surprised to discover the "land he would show us" was Los Angeles, California—not exactly on the top ten list of where this country boy expected to relocate. But true to his character, God's plan was the best, and Kelly and I loved our season of life in L.A. as missionaries.

On one particularly brisk California morning in a garden during my quiet time with Jesus, God reminded me again of those guiding verses from Genesis 12. As I immersed myself in thanking him for his clear guidance, I felt a firm prompting: "Marty, I want you to fulfill the second half of that scripture." I recalled it from memory, "… and all the nations will be blessed through you."

Have you ever attempted to argue with God? I tried, protesting, "Lord, that's not even possible! How could I go to every nation, let alone significantly impact every people group on the planet? How in the world could every nation on earth be blessed through me?" Jesus patiently waited for me to finish my rant, then answered gently in a single word: "Prayer."

I froze for an extended time until the realization began to sink in. I am a child of God, entrusted with authority to move mountains in prayer. If I pray for all the nations on earth, they are *certain to be blessed*!

I rushed back to our home on the missionary training base and grabbed my dusty copy of *Operation World*, purposing to start this project immediately. *Operation World* is a phonebook-thick, comprehensive prayer guide, outlining specific prayer needs for every nation on earth in a calendar year format.[31] I wasn't very far into this commitment when I ascertained what a huge task loomed ahead. It often consumed more than an hour to read and pray meaningfully over each nation slated for that day. The completion of this project required persistence and self-discipline, but by year-end I had prayed for every nation, from Afghanistan to Zimbabwe, along with multiple people groups listed residing in each nation. In fact, I usually did so while cradling my newborn son in my arms for his first bottle feeding early each morning! As that year drew to a close, I felt Father's approval and the assurance that I (and my boy) had indeed blessed all the nations on Earth.

The invitation to bless the nations of the world is not exclusive. I believe it is offered to all who follow Jesus. You might be thinking, *I'm not sure I'm ready to sign up for an hour a day!* If so, I understand and will provide a practical way for you to start: Download the *Joshua Project* app[32] on your smart phone and pray for its single unreached people group of the day. After you pray, click "Praying" to reveal how many others are engaged in prayer with you! It will only require five minutes to read the summary and pray, but the repercussions of that brief, rewarding effort will be felt around the world.

Pray to the Lord of the Harvest

Jesus is the Lord of the harvest and pronounced a counter-intuitive missions strategy—PRAY! I may instinctively want to initiate action, but Jesus said that the work begins with prayer:

> Then [Jesus] said to his disciples, "The harvest is plentiful but the workers are few. Ask the Lord of the harvest, therefore, to *send* out workers into his harvest field." (Matt. 9:37-38)

This presents a big opportunity: an abundant harvest ready for the picking. The fields are ripe with nearly three billion souls who have yet to hear the Gospel!

This also poses a massive problem: a scarcity of workers for the job. In fact, the lost-to-worker ratio among the unreached is roughly 200,000-to-one![33]

The problem is so immense; it requires a radical solution—PRAYER!

What are we to pray? That Jesus himself will *send out* workers—missionaries. But the word that Jesus uses for "send" in this scripture is not a nice word—it's a forceful one. Rather than instructing us to pray that missionaries be "sent" like a letter, he urges us to pray that they be thrust out like a demon from its host! As recorded in scripture, Jesus uttered the word *ekballo*—the same Greek word used in casting out demons. *Ekballo* means to eject, cast out, expel, thrust, and send away. Fine for ridding ourselves of undesirables, perhaps, but this is how Jesus instructed us to pray for *missionaries to be sent*! "Ask the Lord of the harvest, therefore, to *ekballo* workers into his harvest field." (Matt. 9:38)

We can find *ekballo* other places in the Scriptures:

Paul said to the officers: "They...threw us [*ekballo*] into prison ... (Acts 16:37b)

And Jesus entered the temple and drove out [*ekballo*] all who sold and bought in the temple.... (Matt. 21:12a)

Heal the sick, raise the dead, cleanse lepers, cast out [*ekballo*] demons. (Matt. 10:8a)

But if I drive out [*ekballo*] demons by the finger of God, then the kingdom of God has come to you. (Luke 11:20)

One might ask, "Why does Jesus need to *ekballo* missionaries?" Interestingly, it is the same reason that Paul had to be thrown into prison, the money-changers forcefully driven from the temple, and the demons cast out with power. Not one of them *wanted* to go. And honestly, do we? After more than two thousand years of disobedience, it's time for Jesus to *ekballo us*!

Remember, Jesus always desires the best for us. We want ease, but Jesus destines our faith be refined by fire. We want comfort, but Jesus craves for us depth, meaning and significance. We want happiness; Jesus longs to fill us with joy.

As Lou Engle writes in his book *Pray! Ekballo!* "It should come as no surprise that ekballo vehemence is necessary to disrupt the convenient lives of recalcitrant, under-visioned laborers. Everything about world missions threatens our comfort. We greatly love our hobbit holes and insularity. The idea of preaching to people who come to us may get a hearty amen, but going to them? That takes ekballo. Something strong and forceful must grip us. Ekballo molds human will to the divine will, until human labor becomes divine labor, so that earthly kingdoms become divine kingdoms."[34]

Join the 9:38 Prayer Movement

For the past fifteen years the alarms on my watch or phone have faithfully announced 9:38 a.m.—time to pray to the Lord of the harvest. Matthew 9:37 describes the problem of a ripe harvest facing a lack of workers, and the next verse, Matthew 9:38, provides the solution: praying to Jesus to send forth missionaries. Please note that this is the *only* intercessory prayer that Jesus himself commands in scripture.

So, when my daily alarm goes off, I pause whatever I may be up to, launch my Joshua Project app and pray for the unreached people group of the day, calling upon the Lord of the harvest to send workers to reach them.

By joining forces with other prayer warriors, we will tap into the mountain-moving power of Jesus. You will begin to change your world one prayer at a time. You will discover an intimacy with Jesus as you participate in this history-making prayer.

Prayer Makes a Difference

Kelly and I were jarred awake by an Islamic call-to-prayer loudspeaker blaring from directly outside our compact hotel room. When we arrived at Izmir, Turkey on a ten-week mission, our team encountered the desperate need of scores of families whose homes and lives had been devastated by a recent flash flood. As we worked tirelessly repairing homes day after day, Jesus opened doors to minister to Muslims, demonstrating his love through acts of service.

As had become my morning ritual, I rubbed my eyes and ordered Turkish coffee from Kaddeer, the hotel busboy. As I waited for my gritty breakfast beverage I reflected on the testimony I had heard the previous night. We had been invited to join another ministry and together share testimonies at a gathering of Turkish believers and seekers. One young man in the group that I was placed in led off by sharing his unforgettable story.

> I was in my tent during my time of military service, when suddenly I awoke from my slumber. Actually, now that I think about it, I'm not sure if I was actually awake or just dreaming, but it was so real. I arose from my sleeping bag, exited the tent and began to walk to the top of a nearby hill. Something was drawing me in that direction. When I crested the hill I saw a beautiful stone church with a brilliant light shining through the stained glass windows. I was taken aback because I had never seen a 'church' before, only in books.

> I went to investigate the source of the light. I approached the grand wooden doors of this building and gave one a push. It opened wide and I was met by the source of light. In the center of the church was a great throne and seated on the throne was Jesus. He was the source of brilliant light that drew me to this place.

At this point, listening to this young soldier's testimony, I could contain my excitement no longer. "How did you know it was Jesus? Did he say anything to you?"

> Please understand, I had never before heard a story about Jesus! I did not even know that he had died on a cross. But when I saw his face, I just knew who he was. Yes, he spoke, but only one word. Jesus held out both his hands toward me and I noticed deep scars on his wrists. He looked at me with his penetrating loving eyes and simply said, *Come.*

> I somehow found myself back in my tent and wondered what it all meant. I knew that Turkish Christians had a book called the *Ingil.* You call it the Bible. If I could just find an *Ingil* I could better understand this Jesus who invited me to come. So the next time I was in the city I went to every bookstore I could find but not one of them had an *Ingil.* When I made my request at a final bookstore the shopkeeper pulled a simple book with a red cover from his shelf.

I devoured that *Ingil*! I found an address in the back and they sent me a Bible study course to help me in my journey of faith. Now I am so thankful that I have found this group of Turkish believers. I had been following Jesus for two years before I met another believer.

Kaddeer tapped on our door, bouncing my mind from the night before back to the present. Oh yes, coffee! I took my first slurp of the sweet, thick liquid. (Turkish coffee is an acquired taste.) Enjoying my next sip, I considered the connection between this young man's story and the thirty-day prayer guide that our team was utilizing each morning to pray for the Muslim world. By way of this prayer guide we joined with over a million other believers in praying for Muslims to find Jesus. In fact, we had been instructed to specifically intercede that they would receive a *revelation* of Jesus Christ himself! Could I have just encountered in that young soldier an answer to this type of focused prayer? After absorbing his captivating story, I asked other Turks in my small group of twelve whether any of them had ever received a dream or vision of Jesus. Nine hands went up.

In my heart I sensed the answer to my question: I had indeed seen the fruitfulness of specific prayer. When a million individuals pray with one heart for Muslims to see visions of Jesus, Muslims are drawn to the face of God. Even if only one person were to stand in the gap and pray, God responds. Prayer makes a difference!

Please join me and millions of others who pray annually during the season of Ramadan using the Muslim Prayer Guide. Copies are available at: https://www.worldchristian.com

Also, my own missionary organization has partnered with others to develop a new annual prayer guide called, *Fifteen Days of Prayer for the Hindu World*. We seek to raise a million intercessors to call laborers toward an abundant harvest of Hindus for Jesus. Please join us! Prayer guides are available from: https://pray15days.org

Jesus, I want my life to make an eternal impact. May I be obedient to your command to pray to you to ekballo workers for the harvest. I pray that I will also be willing to be an answer to that prayer. Inspire my heart with the faith to believe that prayer makes a difference, so that my commitment to pray will be consistent with my convictions. Amen.

Accomplish It!

- Have you ever considered the powerful impact you can make through prayer? How can you make prayer a daily priority?

- How could you cultivate a greater level of faith as you build your prayer life?

- Set an alarm for 9:38 am to remind you to pray for workers for the harvest. Memorize Matthew 9:37-38 and use it as the basis for your intercession.

- Download the "Unreached People of the Day" app and use it daily when your alarm goes off: https://joshuaproject.net/pray/unreachedoftheday /app

- Make a list on a post-it note of three people who do not yet follow Jesus. Stick it somewhere you will see it throughout the day—such as a dashboard, mirror or computer screen. Pray often and expectantly for those three individuals and be prepared for God to provide witnessing opportunities.

Chapter 8

Tell: God's Life Savers

About one thing I have absolutely no regrets, however, and that is my commitment many years ago to accept God's calling to serve Him as an evangelist of the Gospel of Christ.
— Billy Graham

Having concluded our Vacation Bible School program, my team hurried to fetch tacos from a local stand. While literally climbing into the van I heard Carlos, my Spanish translator friend, hail me from behind. "Wait, Mar*teen*!" ("Martín," as they call me in Mexico.) "Don't leave... come back and share the Gospel with this man."

I turned to greet the burly companion with Carlos. "Martín, this is Salvador," voiced Carlos by way of introduction.

"*Mucho gusto*, Salvador." I offered, extending my hand. Salvador winced as I shook a bit too vigorously for his condition. He wore an unbuttoned collared shirt over a bloodstained T-shirt, covering soaked bandages.

Though curious of his situation, I continued my Gospel presentation as requested, rushed by the awareness of my entire team held up impatiently in a stuffy van. When I shared about Father's love and the forgiveness available through Jesus Christ, Salvador objected. "No Martín, God could not possibly love me. If you only knew what things I have done. There is no forgiveness left for me." His head sank, weighted by shame.

My eyes inquired of Carlos, who filled in the blanks, "Salvador works as a bouncer at a local night club. Last night he got into a fight with two guys that had to be thrown out of the club. The guys were waiting for Salvador when he left and stabbed him with knives: twice in the stomach and three times through the back. He's been to the clinic, but they said that there is nothing they can do for him. His internal bleeding and injuries are too severe. They bandaged him up and released him. To be honest, there is little hope he will survive."

"Oh God, what do I *say*?" I whispered quietly in prayer, "What words of hope can I offer this man?" Immediately, Holy Spirit brought a story to mind, a familiar narrative that I began to share with Salvador, still viewing the dusty ground.

Carlos translated, "Salvador, there was a man in the Bible who felt exactly like you. He lived for himself and committed sins that shamed him. His sinful life caught up to him and he was crucified for the evil things he had done. This man hung on a cross…right next to Jesus."

Upon hearing this, Salvador raised his head, just enough to make eye contact as I continued. "In the final moments before he perished, this criminal called out, 'Remember me, Jesus.' That simple turning of his heart to the Savior was all that was required. As the men hung from spikes, suspended by wooden beams, Jesus looked at that particular repentant man and declared to him a guarantee of eternal life!"

As I brought these words, Salvador's dampened eyes brightened. "If there was hope for that man, perhaps there is still hope for me…"

"I *know* that there is hope for you, Salvador, because I know the Savior," I responded. "Just turn to him. Open your heart to Jesus and receive his love and forgiveness." Carlos then led a simple but heartfelt prayer as Salvador turned his heart toward the Savior. When Salvador uttered, "Amen," and opened his eyes, I saw a complete transformation: the light and peace of Jesus beamed out from deep within his freshly reconciled soul.

Moved to express my genuine happiness, I awkwardly attempted speaking in Spanish, "Salvador, *tu eres mi amigo*." (You are my friend.) "No Martín," he countered. "*Tu eres mi hermano*! (You are my *brother*.) He patted his chest while speaking as he expressed that I had cared enough to share the Gospel with him, and that we are now brothers. Then he unexpectedly pulled me in for a massive hug and kissed both my cheeks, repeating, "Gracias, mi hermano. Gracias."

The van's horn interrupted Salvador's embrace, and there seemed nothing more I could do. I returned one concluding hug, climbed into the van, and never again saw Salvador. Several weeks later, navigating through the same *colonia* in Mexico, I ran into Carlos. I inquired eagerly about Salvador. "No Martín, no one has seen him since that day you were here…I think maybe that he died. Don't be sad, Martín, he did not die alone; he was with Jesus."

Even so, I felt as if I could have done more for Salvador. That night I experienced an acutely vivid dream. I arrived at heaven's gates at the end of my life and faced a long line of individuals, queued up politely to greet me. Yet one large Mexican pushed his way to the front shouting,

"*Hola,* Martín, I'm so happy to see you!" Then crushing me with a huge hug and kissing both of my cheeks he laughed, "Remember your brother Salvador? I'm here because of *you!*"

It occurred to me later that Salvador's name actually means "savior," and I had been privileged to introduce him to his namesake just before he died.

Treasures in Heaven

Jesus counsels us to invest in that which is eternal.

Do not store up for yourselves treasures on earth, where moth and rust destroy, and where thieves break in and steal. But store up for yourselves treasures in heaven, where moth and rust do not destroy, and where thieves do not break in and steal. For where your treasure is, there your heart will be also. (Matt. 6:19-21)

I expect that one of the greatest joys to anticipate in heaven will be encountering those whom we have influenced for the sake of Christ. I suspect that for most, we will be initially unaware of the extent of our impact. The rewards of simply obeying Jesus…!

Once when addressing a Taiwanese youth conference in Southern California, I shared the story of Salvador. I intended to encourage the students to share the Gospel and to live for that which has eternal value, in particular, human lives. At the conference's conclusion I extended an invitation to receive Jesus Christ as Savior and follow him as the Lord of their lives. Although no one in the auditorium stood as requested, I noticed a few hands timidly slipping up behind rows of chairs and silently slipping back down. I led a prayer to receive Christ intended for all who desired to follow him, but remained uncertain of its impact.

After the closing, a group of girls came forward to meet me. Though collectively too shy to talk much, one introduced herself as Evelyn and thanked me for coming. Dismissing themselves, Evelyn placed a neatly folded paper into my hand. The handwriting read:

Marty,

Thank you so much for coming and speaking to all of us at the youth conference. You may never know the full impact of your words, but my life was changed this weekend.

I will be in heaven because of you. I will be one of the many standing with Salvador waiting to greet you.

Your sister, Evelyn

I am continually humbled with the thought that the living God chooses to use us as agents for salvation. Naturally, the enemy wants to steal this honor from us—the greatest joy in one's lifetime—the privilege of introducing someone to the Savior and perhaps even watching that person blossom and grow in Christ. Why should we so often forfeit this blessing? Do we misunderstand the simplicity of the Gospel?

What *Is* the Gospel?

"Gospel" literally means "good news." The essence of this Good News is the historical record of Jesus and why he came. This is why Matthew, Mark, Luke and John's written accounts of Jesus are called "The Gospels." They document the Good News of what Jesus carried out—for you and me!

> Now, brothers, I want to remind you of the **Gospel** I preached to you, which you received and on which you have taken your stand. By this Gospel you are saved, if you hold firmly to the word I preached to you. Otherwise, you have believed in vain.

> For what I received I passed on to you as of first importance: that **Christ died for our sins** according to the Scriptures, that **he was buried**, that he **was raised on the third day** according to the Scriptures, and that he appeared to Peter, and then to the Twelve. (1 Cor. 15:1-5)

The Gospel encapsulates the historical truth that Jesus, the God-man, entered this world as a baby, lived a perfect life, and then offered that life sacrificially in place of our sins. He died, was buried, and rose to life on the third day. He conquered death and now Jesus' life is imparted to us simply by believing in him. When we receive him as our Savior, our fitting and natural response is to follow him wholeheartedly as our Lord and King.

Our Heart Problem

Not until my senior year in high school did I really develop a relationship with Jesus. In the midst of loneliness, confusion and self-destructive behavior, I turned to the Bible to find answers. My honest prayer was *Jesus, if you are real, I want to know you. Please show yourself to me through this book. If it is true, that you want to be my friend, then I want to be yours.* I approached the Bible as if for the first time, searching for friendship with the book's Author. I poured over all the Gospels to rediscover what Jesus undertook as the God-man among us. When I read Luke's account of the crucifixion, I broke down and cried. For the first time I saw my best friend on that cross. Jesus had given his life as a sacrifice for *me*. To this day I remain marked by the significance of that central truth.

Out of my new-found friendship with Jesus I discovered a strong desire to share my faith with others. I wasn't exactly sure how to go about this, but I do remember my big request: "Jesus, before I die I want to lead one person to faith in you."

You might be amused by me regarding this prayer as "big," but it *was* big considering that at this point in my life, I was unaware of anyone that I knew personally who had led someone to Christ. In my Christian upbringing, one might dare invite someone to attend church, but to personally "witness," (share the Gospel with an individual) was practically unheard of. I wondered where, then, this new desire in me to talk openly about Jesus came from. Was the lack of genuine witness in the Christian culture that I had observed completely out of the ordinary? Might our corporate reluctance to share Christ point to a larger heart problem in the Church?

I think that my budding interest in witnessing followed in direct proportion to my growing love for Jesus!

Could our lack of witness reflect a lack of appreciation for what Christ did for us personally? Could our lack of sharing the Gospel be the result of an unkindled relationship with our best friend? "But God demonstrates his own love for us in this: While we were still sinners, *Christ died for us.*" (Rom. 5:8) Jesus died for me though I did not deserve it. If that's not a best friend, I don't know what is.

The world will not be reached for Jesus until this heart problem is resolved. Becoming missionaries will not cause us to suddenly start leading others to the Lord. The desire to share Christ must start right now, right where we live, if it is to extend to the ends of the earth. How can our hearts burn with passion for the unreached in India or Indonesia if we don't kindle the fire of bringing the Good News to our neighbors, classmates, clients, or those we work out with at the gym?

Jeremiah Fire

We need to discover a fire that's ignited by our love for God; like the fire that burned in the heart of the prophet Jeremiah. Imagine being given a mission assignment, and along with it, being issued a warning that the people will not receive your message. Would you still make the effort? Jeremiah ventured out regardless, driven by his love for God and obedience to the King.

> But if I say, "I will not mention him or speak any more in his name," his word is in my heart like a fire, a fire shut up in my bones. I am weary of holding it in; indeed, I cannot. (Jer. 20:9)

Jeremiah's heart blazed so hot that he was incapable of suppressing the truth. God's fire burned from within and Jeremiah was compelled to release it! I have made this my own prayer and invite you to take it for yourself. *Lord Jesus, ignite my heart with Jeremiah's fire so that I will not be able to keep you to myself. Do not allow the enemy to steal my joy of leading others to salvation. Set me free from the fear of man so that I will be free to share your love with anyone.*

Ask God for a Divine Appointment

While finishing this chapter I heard a story from my friend, Madeline, which illustrates what God might do when we make ourselves available to him. Father had been stirring a deep desire in Madeline's heart to lead someone to Christ. "Last night I prayed with desperation for God to put someone in my path who was ready to receive the Gospel," she confided. "Father, I'm tired of just planting seeds, I want to lead someone to Jesus!" Madeline had pleaded with God. "This morning, while driving to work, I saw a woman waiting at the bus stop who was visibly upset. I pulled my car over and offered to pray for her. Surprisingly, she allowed me to pray on the spot, and as I did, her agitation began to melt away. In that moment, I asked if she wanted to have a relationship with God."

The woman looked at Madeline and asked, "Is that even possible?"

At this God-ordained bus stop, Madeline began to share hope and life through the Savior, Jesus Christ, to a desperate heart. The woman responded to Madeline's invitation by opening her heart to Jesus with a simple, "yes." When that single-syllable response crossed the woman's lips she began to describe an overwhelming peace rushing over her.

"That's the Holy Spirit," Madeline assured, "He will always be with you from now on."

Madeline remarked, "I was shocked by how easy it was! All I did was present the simplest Gospel message ever and God did all the work! I was just available to be used by him." From a simple prayer to a divine appointment: God used a willing servant to help a restless soul find the loving relationship with Savior for which she was created.

We can be overwhelmed by the idea of evangelism, when in reality, it is as simple as inviting the Lord to bring about divine appointments and recognizing them when they arrive.

Making Friends

Waiting to hop on my flight out of Burbank one morning, I realized that my boarding card read "15B"—a middle seat. I despise the middle seat, so I waited in the service desk queue to request a new seating assignment. While standing in line I heard the voice of God with clarity. "Marty, don't change your seat; I have a divine appointment for you on this flight."

I nestled obediently into my assigned middle seat beside a woman near the window already pretending to be asleep (it was pretty clear that she wouldn't be my divine appointment), and the aisle seat to my right yet vacant. In fact, the final boarding call had been announced and my divine appointment was still absent. I pulled out my Bible and began to read. *Have I missed something?* I wondered, when at the last possible moment an athletic fellow about my age bustled down the aisle and dropped into my neighboring seat.

"Hi, my name is Marty," I announced, perhaps too eagerly. "Hey, I'm Kevin," he replied, unfolding a newspaper and commencing to read. I became unsure how to proceed, as Kevin did not act eager to converse. "Lord, you are going to have to open a door for me," I prayed silently.

After some time, Kevin slammed his paper against his lap. "I can't believe people. The world is going crazy. Look at this, someone just threw a live baby into a dumpster! They saved the child, but honestly, who would do such a thing!" I nodded in validation of his sudden outburst as he continued. "People don't know the difference between right and wrong these days. There ought to be some standard of truth!"

I could hardly believe the divine setup. "I agree with you Kevin. What do you think that standard of truth should be?"

"I'm not sure about that," and slapping the paper he continued, "something to teach people that you just don't do stuff like this!"

"Kevin, may I tell you what I believe is the standard of absolute truth?" From my lap I lifted the large study Bible that had strangely gone undetected. "I believe that the ultimate standard of truth is found in God's Word, the Bible."

"*Oh no...* you're one of those Bible-thumping Christians," Kevin jeered, unconcerned about masking his disdain. Kevin then launched into a twenty-minute counterattack, pitching questions designed to make any Bible believer's head spin. I determined not to become defensive and, within the barrage, God supplied through me responses beyond my natural store of wisdom. Finally, when Kevin had depleted his ammunition, I spelled out some of the rationale for God's Word being our standard and guide for life.

Before long, the plane descended and I had yet to outline God's simple plan for salvation. As the wheels bumped against the tarmac I mentally whispered a prayer, "Jesus, please give me just a little more time to share the salvation message with Kevin." A petition promptly answered via public address: "I'm sorry folks, but there's going to be a slight delay. Another aircraft is still occupying our gate so we're going to have to wait for them to push back before we can disembark. Sit tight for another twenty minutes or so and we will get you on your way shortly."

"Yes!" I celebrated to myself. Never before had I been thankful for a travel delay. Kevin patiently tolerated my continued presentation. What else could he do? He had petered out of arguments and was retained as my captive audience.

Eventually the cabin doors opened, and I uttered one more thought, "Kevin, I really want to offer you a Bible." Raising mine, I continued, "I would be willing to gift you my very own study Bible, but I would prefer to send you one. Would that be okay?"

"Sure, here's my business card," and he disappeared into the crowd.

I had no way of knowing it then, but at the time of our meeting, Kevin suffered as an alcoholic, his wife had just left him, and his Wall Street company was under federal investigation for white collar crimes.

Soon after my return home, I purchased a leather-bound study Bible just like mine and affixed a yellow Post-it to flag each scripture we had discussed. I mailed it to the address found on his business card, including a personal message. Kevin's name was added to my prayer list—a 3x5 index card I tuck into my Bible.

Two weeks later I worked up the nerve to call Kevin. Ultimately, I figured I held some degree of responsibility toward my "divine appointment."

"Marty... who?" the voice crackled over the line. Which didn't help when I already felt a bit like a stalker.

"Um…you know…the guy you met on the flight a couple of weeks ago…. I sent you a Bible. I was wondering if you received it."

The voice softened only slightly. "Yeah. I haven't read it yet, but I got it. Um…Thanks."

Though a rocky start, I resolved to pray for Kevin every day and to call him or send a card or email every other month—I didn't want to overdo it. In time Kevin began to open up, so I confided that I had been regularly praying for him.

"Well, Marty, it must be working, because I quit drinking. I didn't even go to meetings. One morning I said to myself, *I don't need this anymore.* You know, I probably had four or five drinks already that morning I met you on the plane."

Somewhere in the process, my prayers for Kevin began to change. "Lord, I want to share in the kind of friendship with him that fellow believers have. I don't just want Kevin to be saved, I want to be this guy's friend."

Later over a phone conversation Kevin disclosed that he had reconciled with his wife, Sylvia. I remember he used the word "miraculous." Then in another conversation he informed me that all of his work associates ended up in federal prison. "It's unexplainable, but my case has been suspended and it does not appear that they will prosecute me."

In our exchanges Kevin would agree that *God* was at work in his life, yet he still didn't want to hear about *Jesus.*

After praying for Kevin daily for three and a half years, discouragement settled in. "Lord, after all you've done in Kevin's life, he still doesn't seem any closer to accepting your truth." Very disheartened, I came near to scratching him off my prayer list. "Jesus, I don't think there's any hope for this guy. Can I just take Kevin off my list? Haven't I done enough?"

Jesus' reply came across firm and clear. "I don't want you to stop praying for Kevin; I want you to turn up the heat. I want you to fast and pray until he comes to know me as his Savior." Given how long the process had taken so far, it sounded like a death sentence! I obeyed and started a fast the next day. I even asked the other missionaries at our base to join me in prayer for Kevin's salvation. He was going to get saved, or I was going to starve!

By the end of the week, I resolved to call Kevin and challenge him outright to surrender his life to Jesus. I confronted him, and his response completely shocked me: "I know, I just did that! I gave my life to Jesus Wednesday!"

"What do you mean? How did that happen?" (I kind of wondered if I should feel excited or ripped off that someone beat me to it!)

"Well, at the beginning of this week" (the day I started fasting), "someone gave me a book. I didn't even realize it was a Christian book, but when the main character got on his knees and asked Jesus into his life, I realized that *I* needed to do the same thing. I did it right there on the spot! I knelt down in my office and asked Jesus to be my personal Savior."

I was speechless, tears streaming down my face as I listened.

"My wife Sylvia noticed an immediate change in me and asked, 'Kevin, what in the world has happened to you? Why are you so nice all of a sudden?'"

"I laughed as I told her that I had I asked Jesus to be my Savior earlier in the week… maybe that had something to do with it."

"Hey Kevin," I interjected, "I'm so blown away and happy for you! Here's an idea: let's pray for Sylvia next. Let's pray that she comes to faith in Jesus too."

Before the conversation ended I asked if we could pray together. This time we both prayed, like true brothers in Christ. When the call ended I rushed around the missionary center like a lunatic yelling, "Hey everyone, Kevin just got saved!"

Sylvia started attending church with Kevin and after only a few months she responded to an invitation to receive Jesus as her Savior. Together they started leading their friends, relatives and neighbors to Christ. They were on fire. Kevin even witnessed to some Mormon missionaries!

Before long Kevin started a mountain biking ministry for his Southern California mega church. He was a natural evangelist. Many of the riders that accompany Kevin are Christians while some are not. Their rides break at the halfway point for believers to share testimonies and offer a prayer. The first time I managed to join Kevin on one of these rides, he had signed himself up for the testimony. I squirmed as he gave his embellished version of meeting an over-eager, wild-eyed, Bible-thumping Christian on an airplane who eventually led him to the Lord. He got the biggest kick out of announcing "...and we happen to have the privilege of riding with this guy today!" as all heads pivoted toward me.

God answered both of my prayers for Kevin. He came to faith in Jesus Christ and we remain dear friends to this day. Kevin and Sylvia are even generous financial supporters of Kelly and my ongoing ministry and special missionary initiatives!

The Great Commission begins with each one of us, right where we are. Being prepared to *tell* is a prerequisite to being prepared to *go*. Fueled by an abiding appreciation for what our friend Jesus has done for us, and diligent in prayer, we are prepared and willing to go wherever, to whomever, he would send us. Remember, though, we don't go alone: Jesus promised that he would lead and come alongside us. Let's be lavish with the Good News throughout the whole world until his mission is accomplished.

Jesus, I confess my heart problem: that I have kept you to myself. I acknowledge many reasons for this—not the least, fear or apathy. I ask that you would set my heart on fire like Jeremiah so that I will share your message to those whom you send me. Show me the opportunities that you are opening around me and give me the courage to tell of your love with boldness. I want the whole world to be set ablaze with the truth of the Gospel. May this burn in my heart! Amen.

Accomplish It!

- What is the essence of the Gospel?

- Do you find it easy or difficult to share the Gospel? What are the contributing factors that make it easy or difficult for you?

- The author states a causal relationship between our loving appreciation of Jesus and our desire to tell others about him. What are your thoughts on that idea? If true, how could cultivating your intimacy with God impact your effective witness?

- The story of Kevin illustrates how our witnessing and prayer lives go hand in hand. Is witnessing or prayer stronger in your own life? How might the weaker component be strengthened?

- Read 1 Peter 3:15. What steps could you take to better prepare yourself to share your faith? Who could you involve to grow with together in this area?

Chapter 9

Go: Searching for Jesus' Lost Sheep

Go means a change of location.
— Loren Cunningham

Traveling aboard the colossal Airbus A330 I felt thrilled to be leading a Mission Adventures team to Nepal. Twenty years had passed since Kelly and I ventured on our first mission to this Hindu kingdom, planting Gospel seeds in remote villages that had never heard of Jesus.

As our plane neared Kathmandu International Airport my mind replayed our previous travels. Kelly and I were so young when leading that adventurous troop of trekking missionaries. For weeks our team had endured laborious hikes to remote villages, our backpacks weighted with Gospel booklets. Today there are roads that access each of those villages. What took us weeks to cover on foot back then, would require our present team only days, traveling by bus and jeep. What wonderful, archaic memories!

When *going* becomes a way of life, one's story fills with epic adventures.

The highlight of Kelly and my journey twenty years ago was the precious sibling pair, David (4) and Jasmine (2) who became indelibly interwoven into our lives. Their aged grandmother had pleaded with our team to take her grandchildren; she presumed that she was dying and thus became desperate to secure their ongoing care. Our trekking guide, John, and his wife, Elizabeth, ran a ministry to orphaned and abandoned children, and readily accepted this dying grandmother's request by receiving these two new ones into their home.

My wife and I had once carried these children upon our shoulders, but now upon my arrival at the Kathmandu airport, I encountered a grown-up David who could easily carry me *and* my own grown son, Isaac, who was with me, on his shoulders! David and Jasmine beamed as my team stepped out from the secure arrival area. They were ecstatic to meet my son, hugging and calling him their "American brother." Kelly and I had supported David and Jasmine over the years as they grew up under the loving care of John and his wife. Now I embraced young adults full of passion, life, and the love of Jesus. They both serve as full-time missionaries: David as a gifted evangelist and Jasmine fulfilling her dream to care for children in need. Those once "rescued" and carried away from their remote mountain village, would now guide our team of eighteen students and adults to their place of origin in the Himalayas.[35]

The Gospel is Great News!

After a session of worship the following morning, David dispatched our team on its first assignment. In groups of three or four, he equipped us each with one of the Nepali nationals as a translator, to go out and get our feet wet sharing the Gospel. Though far from unprepared, nervous faces accompanied these young Americans, as if being sent out as lambs among wolves.

Two hours later they returned, ecstatic and loudly chattering over one another. Bill, one of the youth leaders, took the floor with wide-eyed enthusiasm. "We went out and struck up a conversation with literally the first young man we saw. Libby shared her testimony and I gave a simple Gospel message. When Justin asked the young man if he wanted to accept the message and follow Jesus, he looked at us surprised and a little confused. Finally, he blurted out, 'Who would *not* want to accept this? This is great news! In fact, this is the best news I have *ever* heard!' We were able to lead the first person we met to the Lord and gave him a Nepali Bible!"

Bible Power

That morning before our assignment, David had received a treasured shipment—an entire pallet of Nepali Bibles. The teens hoisted one case after another up two flights of stairs to David's apartment. Looking at the stacks of Bibles lying there reminded me of hauling those Gospel booklets on our backs during my trip twenty years ago with Kelly. "Okay everyone, load your backpacks with as many Bibles as you think you can carry," I announced. The guys, of course, made it a contest, attempting to outdo each other, ultimately taking more Bibles than a pack could itself contain. Then they attached gear creatively to the outside of their packs to accommodate their sacred freight.

David had involved himself in the "End Bible Poverty Now" campaign, so our team would be assisting that cause in distributing Bibles to entire villages. Our slogan became "Share the Gospel, give a Bible, pray…repeat." Along the way we would remind ourselves of a scriptural promise:

> As the rain and the snow come down from heaven, and do
> not return to it without watering the earth and making it bud
> and flourish, so that it yields seed for the sower and bread for
> the eater, so is my word that goes out from my mouth: It will
> not return to me empty, but will accomplish what I desire and
> achieve the purpose for which I sent it. (Isa. 55:10-11)

God's Word Will Accomplish its Purpose

We endured the spine-jarring route to Jomsom—roads that one would think twice about driving with a Jeep, much less a bus. Each time we entered a new village, we would settle into a local trekking lodge, then soon venture out in teams of three or four, sharing the Gospel and handing out Bibles all afternoon. In the evening we would project the *Jesus* film at a local school or fellowship using a mini-projector, iPod, Bluetooth speaker and fold-up screen. We saw dozens of Nepali people respond to the Gospel every day in every village we visited.

When Kelly and I had hiked to these same remote, high places twenty years ago we did not encounter a single person who had ever heard of Jesus, nor had any one ever seen a Bible. We couldn't find a single believer, let alone a church or fellowship established this far inland, at over 9,000 feet above sea level. Now, only two decades later, I was amazed to greet believers and identify at least one small fellowship in each of these same villages. God is faithful! The Gospel seeds my wife and I had planted and the prayers of many had taken root and were bearing fruit.

Kingdom Warriors

Arriving in a small village called Kagbeni, we visited the very Buddhist monastery where I had specifically "bound the enemy" so many years prior.[36] Now, the atmosphere felt more like a museum than its former, ominous stronghold of darkness. Interestingly, they were erecting a new temple right beside the old one. We all wondered if this was perhaps because the old one was "broken" along with the enemy's base of operation within it.

Steps of Obedience

We boarded Jeeps in Kagbeni to climb to the high and holy Muktinath, a city name that translates literally, "salvation," and serves for many as a Hindu pilgrimage destination. The steps to the sacred temple felt familiar from my previous ascent. As I climbed, I observed laboring Hindu pilgrims struggling with the incline and I considered the irony. They journey to Muktinath to bathe in water flowing from one-hundred bronze calf heads, in hopes that their sins will be washed away. All the while, true forgiveness has been accomplished by Jesus, through his sacrifice as the Lamb of God, available to all who simply turn to him.

Halfway to the temple, I thought I heard the voice of Jesus say, "Marty, I want you to place a Bible in the foundation." I was surprised by the specific request, not sure how that was even possible. The foundation of this temple was laid hundreds of years ago, and I wondered how it could be accessed? I told Jesus, "If this prompting is from you, I am willing; I just need you to show me when and where it is to be done."

After taking time to respectfully worship Jesus around the Hindu temple, David and Jasmine began to lead us to the neighboring Buddhist monastery. (In Nepal, many make little distinction between Buddhism and Hinduism; often embracing both religions equally at the same time.) On the way we passed by a looming thirty-foot statue of Buddha, still under construction. Workers busily set stones for the plaza but the cut-stone foundation beneath the enormous Buddha itself had not yet been mortared in. I again felt the prompting of Jesus, *Now is the time, this is the place.*

I whispered to Dave, one of the team members, "Hey, can you quickly grab a Nepali Bible and put it in a Ziploc?" He began to question my appeal but noticed my earnest sincerity. Moments later he returned with the sacred item while our team members milled about. I explained the plan, and we soon had honed in on a particular gap between two foundation stones. When we slipped the sheathed Bible between them it dropped down out of sight, *into the very foundation.* I then called the team together for a time of prayer at that place.

"Guys, I'm not sure why, but Jesus just had Dave and I insert a Bible into the foundation of this monument. We are going to pray now that this will not be a place of deception or a stronghold of the enemy, but rather that this city will become a beacon of light of *true* salvation, based in God's Word and found in Christ alone." We had a powerful time of prayer and then continued our journey.

The Power of the Cross

We hiked the quad-burning descent from Muktinath back to Kagbeni, where I welcomed the time to stretch my legs and enjoy the beautiful landscape of Nepal—white-capped Annapurna peaks jutting skyward in praise from behind barren granite ridges. This day had proven so special for me, each place we visited bearing significance from the past. During my early morning quiet time I had made one special request, "Jesus, I would like you to give me one divine appointment today. Provide a person you have ordained to receive the Gospel in a powerful way." God's Word says, "I am not ashamed of the Gospel, because it is the power of God for the salvation of everyone who believes: first for the Jew, then for the Gentile." (Rom. 1:16)

Despite the day's lineup of rich events, it was now drawing to a close without me encountering my divine appointment. While considering this, from the trail below emerged a Nepali man in his mid-twenties, riding on a horse. At his appearance I knew immediately that he was going to be my divine appointment from my morning prayer. I indicated to David that I wanted to talk to the stranger and David forcefully halted the horse and rider. "Please step down, we have something to tell you."

The rider complied and dismounted. We introduced ourselves and learned that this man, Lemcha, had been a Buddhist monk since childhood. He had since abandoned that practice and belief, his life currently out of control in drinking and fighting. "I was just in a fight in that village," Lemcha braggadociously remarked, "No one can tell *me* what to do." Noting the abrasions streaking his hands and face, we didn't doubt it. His bloodshot eyes also testified that he had been drinking.

"We are not going to tell you what to do. We only want to tell you some good news about Jesus," I assured him. I motioned for Justin to bring over his Evangecube,[37] a small toy-like block that unfolds according to a pattern, presenting the Gospel through seven different color illustrations. Justin began by showing the first scene portraying our separation from God and continued by unfolding the cube to the second scene revealing a depiction of Jesus hanging from a cross. When he opened to the second scene, something unusual took place. Lemcha recoiled as if he had been struck in the face by an unseen water balloon. Clasping both hands over his eyes he cried, "No. No! Too powerful!

Take it away. I can't look at it." Lemcha refused to open his eyes until we assured him the image was put away.

His action reminded us of the scripture, "For the message of the cross is foolishness to those who are perishing, but to us who are being saved it is the power of God." (1 Cor. 1:18) Had we just witnessed the visceral reaction of the powers of darkness when they encounter the power of the cross?

We continued to share the Gospel with Lemcha as he listened with intention. Though not ready to give his life to Jesus, I pressed the Bible into his hand, looked into his tired eyes and promised, "This book will change your life. I know, because it changed my life. When you read it, pray and ask Jesus to reveal himself to you. That's what Jesus did for me, and he became my best friend. He wants to be your best friend too." We gathered around Lemcha and invited Jesus to transform his life through the power of the cross.

He mounted his horse and continued his journey up the trail. "I promise. I will begin reading Bible tonight," Lemcha called out in parting. Before getting into his rhythm, he paused to ask David's Nepali friend Sunam, "Is everything that man said true?" "Yes," Sunam replied confidently. "Jesus is God and will change your life."

The Power of Media

The next day we descended by bus to Tattopani, checking into the same trekking lodge that Kelly and my team had stayed in twenty years back. The memories of our previous visit flooded my mind. Unlike the dry tundra of Muktinath's rarified altitude, Tattopani is nestled among thick vegetation and blossoming lemon trees. In this very village, we had met David and Jasmine's grandmother and continued our journey with two toddlers in tow! Presently, while walking in the beautiful garden, Jasmine approached and pulled me by the hand. "Oh Uncle, come, you must meet my auntie—my actual relative."

We approached a Nepali woman with friendly eyes, not too much my elder. When Jasmine made the introduction, the woman and I exchanged knowing looks; this auntie and I remembered each other. Time had been gentle, and though we had both aged, we recalled our previous sighting in which her beloved niece and nephew had been, out of necessity, carried away by strangers.

"Look at us, Auntie." Jasmine implored, "See how good God has been to me and my brother, David. Listen to us as we tell you the story of Jesus. Uncle Marty will show you with his device."

Before the trip I had downloaded the Jesus Film Project App[38] and preloaded every Nepali Gospel film. By contrast, the Spanish *Jesus* movie on 16-millimeter reels—the film that Kelly and I had given to Marlien and Miguel—cost $1,000 twenty-five years ago! Now I possess every translation of the *Jesus* film ever created, along with scores of other evangelistic films *for free*, right on my iPhone! Additionally, we had purchased a portable video projector and sound system to leave with David, which we had been utilizing for evangelism every night. Each *Jesus* showing produced at least a dozen commitments to follow Christ.

Jasmine, Auntie and I sat on a bench in the garden huddled around my iPhone taking in the fifteen-minute Nepali presentation, *Who is Jesus?* At the conclusion, Jasmine summarized the Gospel, then pleaded with Auntie, "Won't you also follow Jesus? Will you also believe in him?"

Auntie had seemed so open to the Gospel, but also genuinely conflicted as she declined the request. Finally she added, "Someday I will follow Jesus, but not today."

"Oh, do you promise, Auntie?" Jasmine inquired. "Do you promise that someday you will follow Jesus?"

"Yes, I promise."

After meeting a second and a third relative of David and Jasmine and encountering a similar response, I decided to ask David, "With so many people all around us coming to faith, why is it that none of your relatives will commit to following Jesus?"

"They are waiting for Grandmother to die," came his immediate response. "You know, she is still alive. She must be a hundred years old by now. She is the oldest person in this region. My relatives feel it would be disrespectful to choose to follow Jesus since Grandmother is matriarch of the family."

"Can we meet Grandmother on this trip?" I inquired. "Can we share the Gospel with her?"

"Yes, definitely we should do that. We will go see Grandmother tomorrow," David committed. "We will share the Gospel with her."

In Search of One Lost Sheep

See that you do not look down on one of these little ones. For I tell you that their angels in heaven always see the face of my Father in heaven.

What do you think? If a man owns a hundred sheep, and one of them wanders away, will he not leave the ninety-nine on the hills and go to look for the one that wandered off? And if he finds it, I tell you the truth, he is happier about that one sheep than about the ninety-nine that did not wander off. In the same way your Father in heaven is not willing that any of these little ones should be lost. (Matt. 18:10-14)

The next day we managed the steep and slippery trail that rose to Grandmother's village. As we hiked through hot sticky air I missed the cool arid climate of the Upper Himalaya. We arrived at a small church nestled in the hillside, where the pastor and his wife welcomed us with lemonade and biscuits. The pastor, a simple man, had come to faith a decade earlier, and moved by the call of Christ, had built a small church on his own property to invite villagers into worship of the one true God.

After recovering from the depleting morning ascent, we were split into teams to canvas the area, share the Gospel, hand out Bibles and offer invitations to our showing of the *Jesus* film that night. My son, Isaac, and I, along with a few others, joined David and Jasmine's team. We already knew our special assignment.

Our small team had shared the Gospel with several persons along the short walk to Grandmother's house. When we eventually arrived at her home, we were disappointed to find no one present. A padlock even secured the door. Where might a hundred-year-old woman have gone? David inquired with one of the nearby neighbors and learned, "She has gone up the mountain, along with her goats."

There was no questioning that we had to find her, but how? Looking up at the thickly vegetated mountainside, it seemed that Grandmother could be anywhere! "Dad, we can track the goats," Isaac suggested. *Not a bad idea.* Isaac has been hunting with me since childhood and has proven to be a proficient tracker. We started up the steep trail, and at frequent intervals found telltale evidence of the goats' direction.

After several hours traversing the lofty terrain we grew increasingly uncertain that we would zero in on Grandmother and her elusive goats. The ground leveled slightly and we perceived that we were nearing some type of summit. Although all goat sign pointed toward a trail to the left, Holy Spirit nudged each of us to veer right. We couldn't explain it. How would we ever find Grandmother if we lost the goat tracks?

We had only traveled a short distance down the chosen path when we approached a small stone home, its inhabitants running out at us yelling, "Jai Masi," a greeting used only by Nepali believers. Jesus had led us directly to a home of believers, and somehow we all shared a strong confirmation that this was exactly where Jesus wanted us in that very moment.

We asked if the family needed prayer and began to pray for their needs, one-by-one. Their fifteen-year-old son had terrible stomach pains and complained of some deformity in his back, the nature of which we were uncertain. We began praying for the boy, believing for his complete healing. We repeatedly stopped to check, "How about now…do you feel any better?" and would commence praying when he indicated that pain was still present. After praying the fourth time, there was no need to inquire. The boy's head jolted up and his wide eyes asked, "What just happened?" We all knew he had encountered the power of God. "My stomach is fine and there is no longer pain in my back," the boy announced, "Jesus has just healed me!"

Immediately I sensed a strong, yet unusual prompting, and had to speak it out. "Isaac, Jesus wants you to speak a prophetic word to this young man and it will come to you as soon as you start talking." Isaac stared at me in shock, but my intense expression told him that I was serious. He took the step of faith. After a few "Um…" false starts, he began by saying, "The Lord wants you to know…" and then words began to flow. Isaac shared a powerful encouraging word that this young man was like the young Samuel of the Bible—that God would call him from a humble beginning to cause a mighty impact in his nation. Everyone present felt a strong sense of Jesus' presence, and our team knew that the Shepherd had directed our steps specifically to encourage this mountaintop family of fellow believers.

Within a short time the mother had prepared sweet black tea and each of us enjoyed our cup as we explained the purpose of our journey up the mountain. "So," David continued, "we are looking for my grandmother. We were told she brought her goats with her and we wish to find her and share the Gospel with her."

"Oh," came the mother's immediate reply, "we know exactly where she is. Follow our son. He will show you the way."

If we needed any further evidence of the boy's healing, we had it, as he sprung into motion and none of us could keep up. We struggled to follow him over a faint trail rising through foliage and into an open field where corn had been planted. David then exclaimed, "Look, on the other side of the field, the old woman with a sickle; that is my Grandmother!"

Reaching Grandmother with the boy's help set off quite a joyful reunion. We were doubly shocked to find that the very Auntie who had promised to someday follow Jesus back in Tatopani was there, and now stood alongside Grandmother waiting to greet us. I'm still not sure how she managed to beat us to the top of that mountain!

I had purchased a lovely purple shawl in the hope that I would be able to meet Grandmother. I removed it from my daypack as we all moved to sit on the crumbling steps of the small stone building and presented it to her. "Grandmother, I want you to know that David and Jasmine are just like family to my wife and me. I consider you my relative and honor you with this gift." I was taken aback at her heartfelt embraces. We also remembered one another from twenty years ago. Translated through David, Grandmother exclaimed, "Look, my son from America has remembered me and has brought me this beautiful gift."

"Grandmother, look, this is my own son, Isaac."

"Oh, I have a grandchild from America!" she exclaimed while cupping his face in her hands.

Then came Isaac's turn to share the Gospel using the simple illustrations on the Evangecube. Both David and I shared key points from the message, urging Grandmother to come to faith in Jesus.

The Lord put a particular scripture on my heart and I began to share it with Grandmother, point by point from memory.

> If you confess with your mouth, "Jesus is Lord," and believe in your heart that God raised him from the dead, you will be saved. For it is with your heart that you believe and are justified, and it is with your mouth that you confess and are saved. (Rom. 10:9-10)

"Grandmother, I want you to believe the truth that Jesus loves you. He died for you and is raised to life so that you can be saved. Will you confess now that Jesus is Lord?" I waited and silently prayed.

An unforgettable moment then transpired: Grandmother bowed her head as David led her in a simple prayer, acknowledging Jesus as Savior and Lord. You could almost hear the celebration in heaven from atop that peak! This one lost sheep had just found her way home.

When the Gospel is living in our hearts we will be Father's ambassadors wherever we go. Jesus is calling you. Will you go? Will you take the greatest news to those who have never heard?

Jesus, if you can use me, I am willing to go. Whether you send me across the street or across the ocean, I want to know the joy of being used by you to reach your lost sheep. Here I am God, send me. Amen.

Accomplish It!

- You are already "going." Whether you go across the ocean or across the street, how can you combine your going with kingdom-minded purposes?

- What examples were given in this chapter of the power of the Gospel multiplied over time? What implications might this have for your own life?

- How could Gospel-sharing tools such as the Jesus Film Project App assist your going?

- Begin preparing now to go on a short-term mission trip. You could even be the catalyst to mobilize a team from your church.

- Prayerfully consider dedicating your life to going as a long-term field worker among the unreached.

Chapter 10

Send: Supporting God's Greatest Work

Go, send, or disobey.
— John Piper

I want to honor the countless number of supporters who contribute toward sending out missionaries. Front-line workers could not go—and could not continue serving—without you!

Your role as sender in equipping, launching, and supporting reflects what the Father did in sending his Son. The following words are familiar, but read them carefully to understand the significance of the sender.

> For God so loved the world that he *gave* his one and only Son, that whoever believes in him shall not perish but have eternal life. For God did not *send* his Son into the world to condemn the world, but to save the world through him. *Whoever believes in him is not condemned*, but whoever does not believe stands condemned already because he has not believed in the name of *God's one and only Son.* (John 3:16-18)

Without the sending of the Father, there would be no going for the Son, and thus no salvation for us! Notice in these words the desperate condition of the world. Those without Jesus are LOST! They are *already* condemned, crushed under the weight of their own sin without a savior to lift it from them. Father did not send Jesus to condemn the world but to save the world through his sacrifice. One must believe in Jesus to be saved. If this were not so, his sacrifice would be meaningless.

Imagine what it cost the Father to send his Son! Accordingly, consider what ultimate value he places on us. Now imagine further the degree that Father longs for his *lost* children, still unaware of his loving sacrifice.

So as a sender, one who sends and supports others, you serve a crucially significant role in bringing fulfillment to the Father's heart for his lost children. By partnering in going *and* sending, we can fulfill the Great Commission and honor the sacrifice of both the Father and the Son.

Sending Churches

When Kelly and I left full-time pastoral ministry to pursue our missions calling, we were neither sent nor supported by our church. We dearly wished it could have been otherwise. As a result, we served as full-time missionaries for a full year without the support of a church body. At that point it became a source of discouragement, as we have always treasured the relationship between church and missions. In frustration, I cried out to God, "Lord, are we truly called by you? If so, why do no churches support our work? Jesus, if you want us to continue as missionaries, I pray that you would confirm our call by providing a church who will recognize us as *their* sent ones." Within a week, two churches in different states informed us that they wanted to regard Kelly and I as their missionaries, and as such would begin sending us financial support. One church began giving $75 per month and the other $25. The amounts were not nearly as significant as God's confirmation to us.

Did you know that the word apostle simply means "one who is sent"? It is perhaps the clearest definition of the word *missionary*. Sent ones carry the word of life to a world in desperate need. Christians have the privilege of endorsing other believers who are called by God as sent ones, through training, encouragement, prayers and financial support.

Sending our Children

At first glance Jim and Patty seemed an odd couple: Jim, a large boisterous Italian New Yorker and Patty, a petite soft-spoken Korean. But they obviously loved each other and they both loved Jesus. I had the opportunity to stay in their Manhattan condominium while on a speaking tour.

One morning while sitting across the breakfast table from Patty, sipping coffee, she began to relate a story about their only son, Jimmy. He had returned from a short-term mission trip with fire in his eyes.

"Mom, I've found my life purpose. I know what I want to do with my life—I want to be a missionary," the young Jimmy told his mother.

"Where did you get such a crazy idea?" Patty responded, "You don't want to be a missionary...you want to be a doctor or a wealthy businessman. You can make a difference by making lots of money and giving it to missions. But you don't need to *go*."

Her story seemed more of a confession as she returned to the present: "Now, years later I recognize that my words deflated my son's life ambition and true calling. Jimmy dropped the whole idea of becoming a missionary, but instead of pursuing other aspirations, he became completely purposeless. He started running with the wrong crowd and got into the whole club scene. Now, as an adult, he's an addict and spends most of his days homeless. I wish there was something we could do to help him." At this point Patty held back tears, "I would do anything to see him as a missionary now. I wonder if things would have turned out differently if I would have only encouraged him to follow his dream."

Sadly, one of the greatest obstacles to the missionary calling can be parents who withhold their blessing. We need to change our view of the missionary vocation. I believe it is the greatest calling to which anyone could ever aspire. It's an obvious sacrifice for parents to entrust their children to God as they pursue the unique challenges of mission work. But Jesus is worthy, both of their decision to go and of our parental decision to send them with our absolute blessing.

Sending our Money

My friend Tom and his wife, Wendy, have made it their personal goal to invest one million dollars in missions. They are not "rich" as one might assume given their aspiration...in fact, Tom's business has struggled, often on the brink of collapse. Their commitment to the Great Commission remains unquestionable.

A few years ago we sent a Bible School outreach to India that connected with a Bible translation effort to bring God's Word to four million Sadri speakers in their mother tongue. Pastor Sadhu had completed the New Testament's translation but was unable to fund the printing. I felt a prompting to reach out to Tom, who mailed a check the next day covering a significant portion of the entire project's cost.

Through that endeavor, Pastor Sadhu and I initiated a friendship, and on a recent trip to India, I had the opportunity to catch up with him and his ministry's progress. As I was leaving he pressed two blue books into my hand saying, "Dear brother Marty, thank you so much for bringing the Word of God to my Sadri people. I want to give you these copies from our first printing in appreciation for your support. This one is for you and this one is for your friend Tom."

Shortly after my return from India I happened to be making a trip to Montana where Tom lived, so I decided to deliver his gift in person. While Tom and I stood outside his home, admiring his old beater pick-up truck, I announced with a sheepish grin, "Oh...I have something for you, buddy." From behind my back I revealed a blue book accented with silver-embossed foreign script, and placed it in Tom's hand.

He looked down at the gift in obvious confusion. Finally, he questioned, "What is it?"

"Tom, that's one of the Sadri Bibles you invested in a few years back. Pastor Sadhu wanted to honor you with a first copy in his appreciation."

Tom's eyes began to well up as he gripped the precious treasure. "Back when you asked, we had the money to give, so we gave it. After that, we lost everything. I would have lost that money too had I not invested it in this project. This is all I have left from that season."

The money we send to complete the Great Commission is an investment in God's kingdom. It can never be taken away.

Sending Indigenous Workers

A great strategy for sending can be to financially support indigenous workers. These foreign nationals, trained and already living in the field, know the culture and the language. Living near unreached people groups, these missionaries can be quickly mobilized but need support in order to dedicate their time fully to evangelism and church planting.

Keep in mind some of the statistics from chapter 5. For every thirty missionaries sent to those within reach of the Gospel, we have dispatched only one missionary to the unreached. (See Appendix, Figures 1 and 4.) Sending indigenous workers is a strategic way to shift that balance. Grassroots organizations such as Harvest Frontiers and the Timothy Initiative are flipping those statistics on end by sending nearly 100% of their nationals to work among unreached peoples. It is one of our greatest joys and privileges for my wife and I to meaningfully support seven indigenous workers among the unreached, even on our own missionary income.

Sending Ourselves (When Sending Becomes Going)

Remember Kevin from chapter 8? Shortly after he and Sylvia came to Christ, they began to recognize the value of what Kelly and I do vocationally, and unprompted, began supporting our ministry. Once, while enjoying a jovial phone conversation about mountain biking and hiking as friends do, I made an off-handed comment, "Hey Kevin, you know what you should do? You ought to join me on my next trip to India."

"Marty, I can't do that, I don't have a passport. You know I'm still under a federal indictment and they seized it—I won't get it back unless those charges are dropped."

"What if you *did* have a passport? *Would* you go with me?"

"Okay Marty, if my charges get dropped and I get my passport back, I'll go with you to India, but I don't see that happening any time soon—if ever."

"Do you promise—I mean, if you get your passport back, Kevin—do you promise to come with me?"

"Oh boy…" he sighed. "Yes, I promise."

"You know that I'm going to pray that you get your passport back, right?" I ribbed him.

"Ha! That's what I'm afraid of. When's your next trip to India?"

"In two months." After the conversation ended, I added, "Kevin's Passport" to my prayer list.

A few weeks later Kevin phoned. I answered to hear his opening line, "Well, it looks like I'm going to India!" His charges had been expunged and so he received his passport, booked his ticket, and joined me on an unforgettable adventure.

Be prepared: your sending can ironically become going!

Father, thank you for leading by example in your willingness to send your only Son, Jesus, as a missionary to us. Teach me to be a generous sender. Help me to be a faithful supporter of missionaries, a sender of my money, my prayers and even my children. I'm willing for my sending to become going. Show me how to be faithful each step of the way. Amen.

Accomplish It!

- Find out what missionaries your church supports and send them a care package along with letters of appreciation. Then mark your calendar to do this quarterly.

- If your church has a missions board, volunteer to serve on it. Give a copy of *Mission Accomplished* to your pastor and each member of that board.

- Use *Mission Accomplished* to start a study group in your church, small group or homeschool association. Available in bulk from https://epicfaith.net.

- Actively support both short-term and long-term mission efforts.

- Support indigenous work among the unreached through organizations such as Harvest Frontiers (https://www.harvestfrontiers.org).

- Start a prayer group through your church or cell group to intercede for the needs of missionaries around the world.

Chapter 11

Stay: Our Call to Incarnational Mission

God had only one Son and he made that Son a missionary.
— David Livingston

We believers have the wonderful privilege to take part in accomplishing God's mission. I am profoundly thankful for mission trips I have led and for the teams that have served with me, sharing the Good News of Christ. But we must realize that the Great Commission will not be completed through short-term efforts alone. Mission accomplished will require culture-penetrating, language-learning, church-planting, long-term missionaries! God needs men and women willing to shed their own cultural identity, relocate, and live among the people they are called to reach with the Gospel. Missionaries who will not only *go*, but also *stay*!

> "Going" is easier than "staying." Often, the challenge is not merely to go, but to develop a viable long-term Christlike presence among those who have yet to hear the Gospel clearly. What is required of us is not a casual or temporary response to Christ's command, but a radical lifelong commitment. The result of that kind of commitment is the Gospel taking root deeply within the host culture, wherever it may reside.[39]

I call this "Incarnational Missions" because we become a representation of Jesus to the lost. We must go and dwell among the unreached to communicate the Gospel message through our lives. Perhaps you will become one of these significant sojourners.

Go Means a Change of Location

One reason that I love taking short-term mission teams is because inevitably, some of those individuals become long-term missionaries. Most long-term field workers began their life's adventure on a short-term outreach.

Loren Cunningham, founder of Youth With A Mission, has said, "*Go* means a change of location." Loren practices what he preaches, having walked in every country on planet earth within his lifetime, including many of the island states as well. As a pioneer, he considers his "going" as a prophetic act that paves the way for long-term missionaries to go—and to stay. The international missionary organization that he and his wife Darlene founded now covers the globe!

Responding to the Call

My good friend, Mike, left a high-paying yet soul-draining career, deciding to try something radically different. He joined one of our Discipleship Training Schools and traveled to India for the first time with a small team on a ten-week outreach. Mike adapted well, loved the people, but more than anything, his soul came alive with fresh purpose.

Upon returning from that short-term outreach, Mike committed to join our Idaho team. I can recall one of his greatest obstacles to a long-term commitment: giving up his Texas driver's license, which represented his cultural identity. Relinquishing that coveted laminated card began his transformation; choosing to become like those he was called to reach with the Good News.

When challenged to blaze the way for a new ministry, Mike welcomed that tug on his heart to step forward. Our stateside team commissioned him to relocate to North India where he launched an English learning center. Through this approach, Mike lived among the people, established meaningful relationships, and in time, saw some of those he interacted with embrace the love of his Savior. Mike's enduring commitment to this people group, however, made it difficult for him to find a life partner from his home culture who would join with him in this endeavor.

Bhawna, a lovely, lively Indian lady became one of the first to follow Jesus through Mike's ministry. When I visited Mike with a short-term outreach team, we saw clearly that something special was budding between the two. Soon, an arrangement was made with her family, and I returned to India by invitation as an honored guest at their wedding. What a joyful privilege!

Bhawna was one of the first from her unreached people group to follow Jesus. She was the first believer from her village and the first among her immediate family. On a recent visit to northern India, I had the special privilege of accompanying Mike and Bhawna to her village, and was blessed to be a welcomed guest in her parents' home. I walked with Bhawna's father admiring his farmland, laughed and played games with her brothers, enjoyed her mother's cooking, and built precious relationships with them. Missions multiplies family.

> "I tell you the truth," Jesus replied, "no one who has left home or brothers or sisters or mother or father or children or fields for me and the Gospel will fail to receive a hundred times as much in this present age (homes, brothers, sisters, mothers, children and fields—and with them, persecutions) and in the age to come, eternal life. But many who are first will be last, and the last first." (Mark 10:29-31)

We don't go to the mission field to find a spouse, and that was not Mike's intention. But remember, the character of God is good, and he is more than able to provide for *all* our needs—certainly including a fulfillment as important as a supportive soulmate.

When God does call you to go on a long-term assignment, take the time necessary to prepare. Most mission agencies have a unique field-bound training process. Make the most of your preparation so that you will remain healthy and sustainable in the field. Though transplanted, your new roots will nourish a life budding with fresh relationships.

Incarnational Missions

Incarnational mission is actually what Jesus modeled to us by example. In the first chapter of John's gospel, the disciple refers to Jesus as "the Word."

> In the beginning was the Word, and the Word was with God, and the Word was God. He was with God in the beginning. (John 1:1-2)

Then John explained that Jesus is not only Creator of all things, but that he is the source of light to all people.

> Through him all things were made; without him nothing was made that has been made. In him was life, and that life was the light of men. The light shines in the darkness, but the darkness has not understood it. The true light that gives light to every man was coming into the world. (John 1:3-4, 9)

Next, we see the "missionary relocation" assignment that Jesus received: to descend from heaven (go) and live among those in the very world he created (stay).

> He was in the world, and though the world was made through him, the world did not recognize him. He came to that which was his own, but his own did not receive him. (John 1:10-11)

The message that Jesus brought and demonstrated in person invited all whom he encountered into a reconciled relationship with the Father. That was, and is, the prevailing purpose for which Jesus came—his incarnational mission.

> Yet to all who received him, to those who believed in his name, he gave the right to become children of God—children born not of natural descent, nor of human decision or a husband's will, but born of God. (John 1:12-13)

Get ahold of this phenomenon: the incarnational mission work of the Christ. He became one of us—to reach us! The incarnate presence of Jesus revealed the Father in the most tangible way to the peoples of earth.

> The Word became flesh and made his dwelling among us. We have seen his glory, the glory of the One and Only, who came from the Father, full of grace and truth. No one has ever seen God, but God the One and Only, who is at the Father's side, has made him known. (John 1:14, 18)

Jesus' demonstration of incarnational mission work to humankind now serves as the example for us to follow. Father sends us as his incarnate messengers to represent Christ to a lost world.

> Jesus said, "Peace be with you! As the Father has sent me, I am sending you." (John 20:21)

> [Jesus] who, being in very nature God, did not consider equality with God something to be grasped, but made himself nothing, taking the very nature of a servant, being made in human likeness. And being found in appearance as a man, he humbled himself and became obedient to death—even death on a cross! (Php. 2:5-8)

We can expect that our incarnational mission calling will require sacrifice, but our surrender is well invested when in obedience to the King.

Relocate

To ensure that we don't assume that this type of missionary calling is strictly for young people, I would like to introduce you to one of my personal heroes, Pastor Puna.

At forty years of age, Pastor Puna was struck by the preeminence of the Great Commission. One day Puna was overcome with gratitude for the pioneering missionaries that had brought the Gospel to his people group in Nagaland.

In 1880, Baptist missionaries expanded their work to the northeast corner of India to the Nagaland state. They effectively preached the Good News, with Pastor Puna's great grandfather being among the first to receive the message and follow Jesus as Savior. In his epiphany, Puna wondered what might have happened if those missionaries had never come. How would their lives have been without Jesus? He shuddered at the thought.

A radical idea was conceived in him. What if I were to take the Gospel to a people group without a single believer just as those missionaries brought the Gospel to my people? Before long Puna became convinced that Jesus had spurred this thought and set out to find a people group who had never heard the Gospel—not even once.

With quick success, Puna discovered the Amri Karbi people, hidden in the hills of the northeastern Indian state of Asaam. They had never heard the Gospel and not one known person had ever tried to reach them. From that time Puna made it his personal ambition to reach this people group for Christ. He returned to his home in Nagaland to receive theological training and to be legitimately sent by his church for the work. Then he relocated with his family for his cross-cultural incarnational assignment from Jesus.

My missionary friend, Jonathan, introduced me to Pastor Puna twenty years after he had moved to Assam. I enjoyed the privilege of a day trek across his mission field. At daybreak we began hiking red, muddy trails through vast expanses of vibrant green foliage. As we walked, Pastor Puna related the entire story of his calling and his ministry.

"It was very difficult work at first. I had to learn the Karbi language and customs. I had to build trust among them. In the first year, one man decided to follow Jesus and became like a brother to me, joining with me in God's work. Then, some of the youth were inspired to accept Jesus as Lord. The work continued to grow slowly in those beginning years… that is, until they started killing us."

His statement took me aback, unsure if I had heard him correctly. "Excuse me, Pastor Puna, did you say that the Karbi people began killing the believers?"

"Yes," Pastor replied solemnly. We happened to arrive at the very site as he came to this part of the story. He stopped mid-trail and pointed. "He was my first disciple—my brother. We found his body there, by the trail. His head was found over there on the other side of the creek."

I was stunned, but my new friend did not linger there. As we continued hiking his expression turned to joy. "When the people saw that we would not abandon our faith in Jesus, not even in the face of death, so many more began to accept the message. We could not build churches fast enough to hold all the people who were coming. We continued to have more martyrs for the faith, but so many more came to know Jesus as their Savior."

By this time we arrived in the first village where a church had been planted. Despite simple bamboo construction with a thatched roof, it offered enough room to easily seat a hundred worshipers on woven mats. When those in the village saw us approaching, they began shouting and running to greet Pastor Puna, generating the atmosphere of a celebration parade. I wondered whether the apostle Paul may have been similarly greeted by beloved believers of churches he had established.

We were forced to sit down and drink tea and eat freshly picked miniature bananas that I found to be the sweetest I had ever tasted. Although Puna was sixty-five years old, and skinny as a rail, he devoured plate after heaping plate of rice. When he noticed my astonishment at his consumption abilities he whispered, "My secret is the chilies." Then taking another nibble from a fiery, slender pepper, he chortled, "If I have chilies, I can eat much rice." There was no time to rest after our spicy, starchy lunch and soon we were off and hiking again.

I've always prided myself in staying in shape, but found it difficult to match the pace of this nimble-bodied senior pastor. Each village we came to brought a repeat of the last—another celebratory Pastor Puna parade, more tea and bananas, and of course, burgeoning plates of rice and chilies.

We must have visited a dozen villages with as many churches by the time evening fell, when we finally arrived at "yellow church." Unlike the others, it had been fashioned with brick and mortar, and yes, painted lemon yellow. Locals built a welcoming fire in the courtyard to accompany our concluding banquet of chilies and rice. As we rested around the glowing embers I admired my new friend, Pastor Puna.

"You know, Pastor..." I began, interrupting the silence, "you may well be the richest person I know."

"Oh really?" He smiled in bewilderment, not sure the term applied to him.

"Just consider the riches of these relationships and the great inheritance of the churches you have planted. Yes, I'm sure of it: You are the richest person I know."

I recalled God's promise in Psalms chapter 2:

He said to me, "You are my Son; today I have become your Father. Ask of me, and I will make the nations your inheritance, the ends of the earth your possession. (Ps. 2:7-8)

This hero of faith had the courage to ask something glorious of the Father, and in return Father gave Pastor Puna a nation, an unreached people group, as his inheritance!

Unclaimed riches await you and me. As you respond to Jesus' call to go, to relocate, to become a missional incarnation to those who long for Father's message of life, you will also receive the reward of a life rich with relationship, joy, pain, authenticity, and heavenly inheritance beyond your understanding.

Jesus, thank you for being a missionary to us—for relocating and being a living demonstration of the Father's love. Without you, Jesus, we would never know the joy of our relationship with the Father. Now, give me the opportunity to do that for someone else. Teach me to be the Father's incarnate presence to those in desperate need...even to a people group who has never yet heard of you. Give me courage, and help me remember that I am never alone. Amen.

Accomplish It!

- Your incarnational mission is to be a representative of Jesus to those around you, regardless of where you are called. How will this awareness impact the way you live as an example of God's love?

- Follow Pastor Puna's example and make yourself available to the Father to go and stay among a people with little or no exposure to the Gospel.

- Read Psalms 2:7-8. How could you ask for an inheritance of a nation (an unreached people group) whether you go, stay or pray?

Chapter 12

Multiply: Church-Planting & Disciple-Making Movements

For the earth will be filled with the knowledge of the glory of the LORD, *as the waters cover the sea.*
— The Prophet Habakkuk

Ganesh carefully unfolded a large map as his wife, Sasha, smiled and nodded. They had been attending a pioneering school that we were hosting in an Uttar Pradesh city (a north Indian state). Ganesh and Sasha wanted to meet with me to describe their intended pioneering project. With the map now flat on the table, Ganesh explained that it detailed his central Indian home district—about the size of an average U.S. county.

A God-Given Vision

"Marty, there are 140 villages in the entire district. None of these villages have a church," Ganesh continued, his intensity beginning to rise. "Our goal is to plant a church in *each one* of the 140 villages!"

Though initially thinking this goal sounded overly ambitious, I tried not to let my face show it. Then again, *why wouldn't Jesus want to establish a church in each one of these villages?*

"You wonder how we plan to do this?" Ganesh surmised my hesitancy and continued, now getting to the exciting part. "We will begin to build trust and recognition by offering hygiene programs for the school children and literacy programs for adults. Most adults from these villages cannot read or write, especially the women. We will begin by working in five villages so that we can visit a different village each day of the workweek. We will also begin a simple church in each village on the day we visit them."

"Um, excuse me Ganesh, but I thought you said that there were no churches, no believers in these villages. How will you host a simple church?" I inquired.

"You know Marty, our small team will sing a song, then tell a Bible story, someone will give their testimony, and then we will pray for the sick. Simple church is for everyone. You don't have to be a Christian to come, we will start this right away." Ganesh patiently instructed.

"Oh, okay…that sounds great…" I affirmed, though too embarrassed to admit that the thought of holding "church" for non-believers was completely foreign to me.

"You may still wonder, how we will start 140 new churches in 140 different villages with just our small team?" Ganesh queried, obviously delighted to pose, then answer his own questions.

Why yes, that's exactly what I was wondering. The student was schooling the teacher, so I just smiled and nodded for him to continue.

"We will use multiplication to accomplish this," Ganesh's excitement accelerating to full tilt. "We will work in these five villages for two to three years until we have baptized new believers who can continue their own simple church. Then we will start in five new villages, while each of the first five villages will also have the responsibility of reaching one new village in two to three years. In this way we will reach all 140 villages in just five generations."

Ganesh could tell that he had lost me again, so he explained, "I don't mean generations like grandfather, son, and grandson; I mean, each time a church plants another church, that is one generation. Each generation, the total number of churches will double because every church is *expected* to multiply. When my team plants a church, it is always a "first generation" church, but when that church plants another church it is a "second generation" church, then "third generation" and so on. We can have a new generation church every two or three years, so it might take fifteen years to reach all 140 villages."

At his fiery-eyed conclusion, I sat dumbfounded, purposefully avoiding being a voice of discouragement. (I had known well-meaning pastors using traditional church planting models who labored fifteen years to plant just *one* church, let alone 140.) Yet I had known Ganesh and Sasha long enough to trust that they had a contagious love for Jesus, and that their dedication to him was unquestionable. "I believe in you both and sense that God has given you this vision. My prayers will be with you as you launch this kingdom-expanding work. I am so excited to see what Jesus will do through you!"

Church Planting Movements

Upon returning home, and inspired by Ganesh's vision, I researched and discovered that Ganesh and Sasha's goal is not unrealistic, as what is now referred to as a "Church Planting Movement." David Garrison, author of *Church Planting Movements*, defines it as, "a rapid multiplication of indigenous churches planting churches that sweeps through a people group or a population segment."[40] Garrison and others have been researching church planting movements for nearly two decades to discover how they happen *and* how traditional practices often inadvertently *keep* them from happening. They have documented this type of rapid kingdom expansion on nearly every continent. According to Victor John in *Mission Frontiers*, "God had done far more than we could ask or imagine in starting more than 600 modern-day 'Book of Acts' type movements, with most of them among unreached people groups."[41]

So would I soon see a church planting movement through the ambitious vision of Ganesh and Sasha?

The Power of Prayer

I visited Ganesh and Sasha about a year later along with my friend, Titus, who was in the process of relocating to India as a long-term field worker with his family. We arrived eager to take part in their emerging ministry. Titus and I overnighted in a nearby guesthouse, as Ganesh and Sasha's rented apartment was already bursting with newly joined team members. In the morning we packed into the living room of their cozy flat.

"Before we go out to the village today, let's take some time to pray and ask Jesus to prepare the way for us," Ganesh announced, more for our sake, as the team seemed already eager to pray. Various members prayed out loudly and passionately in their mother tongue. Others read from their Bibles as they prayed. Though Titus and I could not understand their words, we recognized that we were storming the gates of hell on behalf of the lost, and wholeheartedly joined in.

Simple Church with Nonbelievers

After an intense hour in prayer, we piled into a rented Jeep, the driver impatiently lurching forward, clearly knowing his way. We zipped through the city and into open fields dotted with workers and meandering water buffalo. Pavement gave way to gravel, then reduced to crusty ruts in the dirt as we neared the village. Children greeted Ganesh's team, excited for their arrival.

Titus and I hung back and observed the team members conversing naturally with the locals. After a while groups gravitated toward the steps of a cinder block home, fronted with a slightly larger porch than other buildings. Dilli, a young team member, pulled out a guitar and began strumming, singing a happy tune, while young and old joined in. After a few songs, Sasha began a dramatic retelling of a Bible story, apparently of Jesus calming the storm. Next, another member of their team obviously shared a personal testimony in rising and falling tones.

It sure looked like "church" in session, though Ganesh had clearly stated that this village did not yet have *any* Jesus believers. The team approached the event so non-religiously that villagers did not equate it as a spiritual ceremony, only as something authentic that they were happy to partake in.

Jesus Calls Us to Heal the Sick

After the testimony Ganesh explained to Titus and me that we would be praying for the sick, and invited us to actively participate with that segment. Ganesh made the announcement, which quickly produced a line-up behind the porch steps. One-by-one each was asked what he or she wanted Jesus to do, and then we laid our hands upon that person, inviting God's healing touch. One elderly woman came forward nearly doubled in half, unable even to stand up straight. When Ganesh asked what prayer she wanted, she replied so emphatically that he chuckled as he translated for us, "What do you think I want prayer for?! Look at me! I have to live my whole life bent over like this...." We laid hands on the woman and prayed earnestly for healing from Almighty God. She hobbled off and we began praying for the next person. We had just finished praying for the last person when the elderly woman made her way again to the front and addressed the crowd. Standing nearly straight and gazing at them eye-level she exclaimed, "Look at me now! Look what Jesus has done for me! I can stand up straight—for the first time in years! Thank you all for your prayers in Jesus' name!"[42]

We marveled, and I recalled the promise of Mark 16:20, "Then the disciples went out and preached everywhere, and the Lord worked with them and confirmed his word by the signs that accompanied it."

Shortly after the woman's impromptu testimony, Vishnu, the village leader, approached Ganesh and began speaking with him sternly. I wondered what he had said, so Ganesh interpreted, "Why do you meet outside like this? You should have a proper place. The next time you come here, I want you to meet inside my home. There will be enough room for everyone."

Removing Cultural Barriers

Later that week, Ganesh had another visit planned to this very village, so, as requested, we met in Vishnu's home. Sasha had gone ahead with another female team member to conduct the literacy program. When we arrived, all the women were assembled, each with a fragment of chalk and a small chalkboard. Vishnu's wife stood to meet me, excited to show off her new skill. "Look, I have written my husband's name!" she exclaimed in choppy English. Meanwhile, Vishnu's chest swelled with pride at his wife's accomplishment.

I was hard-pressed to ignore the virtual Hindu temple in Vishnu's home. Pictures of Hindu gods hung on every wall, adorned with whispering sticks of incense. Each corner housed a grotesque statue smudged red with paste from the daily punja offered to it. *This is sure a strange place to have "church."*

I discerned also an image of Ganesh, the Hindu god with a human body and the head of an elephant. I had wondered why my church planting friend had kept this popular Indian name for himself. Many former Hindus who become Christians will choose a biblical name such as David, Peter or John. "Why hadn't Ganesh?" I asked Jeremiah, one of my closest seasoned field-worker friends. He explained it this way, "When a believer from a Hindu background goes to a new place and says, 'Hi my name is Peter,' the Hindus will interpret that to mean, *This fellow has converted to Christianity and has abandoned his family's culture. We should be suspicious of him.* But when he says, 'Hi my name is Ganesh' they think to themselves, *Wait a minute; I thought this guy was a Christian. Is it possible to follow Jesus and yet maintain our cultural identity? Maybe we can learn from him.*"[43]

We continued as before in Vishnu's shrine-laden home with a song, a Bible story and a testimony. This time when we initiated prayer time for the sick, Vishnu introduced his son Banu, dressed in a bright orange-collared shirt. "Pray for my son," Vishnu demanded. "Look at the large unsightly lumps on the back of his neck." They appeared to be some form of cysts. This time we prayed out together for all who had indicated a desire for healing. Since Titus stood closest to Banu, he placed his hand directly on the protruding bumps. Later Titus told me, "Marty, it was crazy! I put my hand right on those lumps and when we all started praying, I could feel them moving around underneath my touch. You saw it, didn't you? When I took my hand away, the cysts were gone!" Sure enough, I had seen it, and so did everyone else!

To my present knowledge, Vishnu has yet to become a believer, but when Banu wanted to follow Jesus and attend a special Bible training that Ganesh recently offered, Vishnu gave no objection. He had witnessed firsthand the reality of Jesus at work—right within the walls of his own home. Ganesh and Sasha are not focused on just winning individuals to the Lord but whole families, so that entire communities can be impacted. They avoid rushing a person to make a decision for Christ so that in the discipleship process entire families can be included in the journey toward following Jesus. Because of Ganesh and Sasha's transparent approach, they have established trust among the village elders. Nothing was done in secret, as they had nothing to hide.

Jesus Devotees Receive Water Initiation

When I returned two years later, all five of the initial villages indeed had believers among them, and three already had multiplying fellowships. Furthermore, their team, as planned, had already taken on another five villages. Ganesh and Sasha had baptized newly believing young couples from three of the first villages and appointed them as simple-church leaders. Those couples began to baptize any new followers in their respective villages. In doing so, however, they do not use the term "baptism," with its inflammatory connotation in the Indian culture. Instead they use a local term that translates as "water initiation."

Rather than becoming a "Christian," with all the cultural baggage and misconceptions it implies, Ganesh encourages the title, "Follower of Jesus" or "Jesus Devotees," to simply mark that one is a devoted follower only of God-Jesus.

A westerner may perceive this as "watering down the Gospel," but to these New Jesus Devotees, the titles weigh profoundly rich with meaning. They borrow from language they relate to, bringing understanding and new-found insight.

To date, the work Ganesh and Sasha have initiated has resulted in more than 650 believers among twenty-five churches in sixteen villages. In fact, their progress has already achieved three generations, meaning that some of the first planted churches have initiated new churches themselves, and these resulting churches have also pioneered churches. This would not yet be regarded as a Church Planting Movement with explosive growth sweeping through the entire people group, but as the momentum increases it is prayerfully headed that direction.

We will falter in completing the Great Commission simply by increasing old practices that, in reality, are not keeping pace with today's world population growth. We need to trust Jesus for rapidly reproducing church planting movements like the work that Ganesh and Sasha are igniting and continue to fuel in central India. "These movements are the only way we have found historically for the kingdom of God to grow faster than the population. Without them, even good ministry efforts result in losing ground."[44]

If this type of multiplication sounds to you like something only applicable to frontline field missionaries, may I suggest that you visit the Zúme Project (https://zumeproject.com) and start putting this powerful multiplication principle to work in your home community through your existing relationships? Or read *Contagious Disciple Making* and begin working toward a disciple making movement right where you live.[45] For those working among or witnessing to Muslims, I recommend *Stubborn Perseverance*.[46] (See ad in the Great Commission Partners section for details.)

Father's desire is for every grand metropolis and every remote village to host vibrant, authentic worship directed to Jesus, the Lamb of God, who purchased souls from every people group with his blood. He is the one worthy of worship resounding from every tribe and language in every place on earth!

Jesus, I want to see you worshipped and glorified. Ignite my prayers with faith to believe you for a great end-time harvest. Show me how to engage with the work you are doing around the world, to see your mission accomplished for the glory of your name! Amen.

Accomplish It!

• Continue learning about mission accomplishing issues by visiting Mission Frontiers and subscribing to their quarterly journal and e-newsletter: http://www.missionfrontiers.org.

- Visit the Zúme Project (https://zumeproject.com) and register to start your own Zúme training with a group of friends.

- Identify people living near you who are from unreached people origins. Use resources available through https://internationalproject.org and http://dbsguide.org to start a Discovery Bible Study among them.

- Support those multiplying Disciple Making Movements among the unreached through organizations such as The Timothy Initiative (https://www.ttionline.org).

Part 3: Empowered for His Purpose

Prayer lays hold of God's plan and becomes the link between His will and its accomplishment on earth. Amazing things happen, and we are given the privilege of being the channels of the Holy Spirit's prayer.

— Elisabeth Elliot

Chapter 13

Authorized to Go

Expect great things from God; attempt great things for God.
— William Carey

In the old Westerns, one could easily recognize the sheriff, the one with the badge. The emblem announced that he was the one in charge. Modern men and women in uniform also carry a badge to authorize their power. If you are caught speeding, traffic police will write a citation. Drive intoxicated, and they will haul you to jail. If you endanger someone's life, a person in uniform's authorization may involve deadly force. Paul, the apostle, spoke of the authorities this way:

> "For he is God's servant to do you good. But if you do wrong, be afraid, for he does not bear the sword for nothing. He is God's servant, an agent of wrath to bring punishment on the wrongdoer." (Rom. 13:4)

Those in authority don't have to ask permission; it has already been granted.

Did you know that Jesus has *authorized* you and me to carry out his mission on earth? He gave us his power and told us to use it accordingly. We have been given the greatest mission ever, and along with it, the authority to accomplish that assignment. We are authorized to go!

Authority to Accomplish the Great Commission

Whenever the Great Commission is mentioned within the four gospels, we see Jesus' impartation of authority to accomplish the task! The gospel of Matthew shows us clearly that Jesus holds *all* authority. Jesus has the authority, therefore he is able to grant it to us, his disciples, for the effective accomplishment of his purpose.

> Then Jesus came to them and said, "*All authority* in heaven and on earth has been given to me. *Therefore* go and make disciples of all nations…" (Matt. 18:18-19a)

In his gospel, Mark clearly connected our calling with our authority. He promised that Jesus himself would be working alongside of us!

> [Jesus] said to them, "Go into all the world and preach the Good News to all creation. Whoever believes and is baptized will be saved, but whoever does not believe will be condemned. And these signs will accompany those who believe: In my name they will drive out demons; they will speak in new tongues; they will pick up snakes with their hands; and when they drink deadly poison, it will not hurt them at all; they will place their hands on sick people, and they will get well." After the Lord Jesus had spoken to them, he was taken up into heaven and he sat at the right hand of God. Then the disciples went out and preached everywhere, and the Lord worked with them and confirmed his word by the signs that accompanied it. (Mark 16:15-20)

Doctor Luke used similar language in both his gospel and his history of the Acts of the Apostles. He recounted first what Jesus told his disciples to say, and then how he gave them the power to say it!

> [Jesus] told them, "This is what is written: The Christ will suffer and rise from the dead on the third day, and repentance and forgiveness of sins will be preached in his name to all nations, beginning at Jerusalem. You are *witnesses* of these things. I am going to send you what my Father has promised; but stay in the city until you have been *clothed with power from on high*." (Luke 24:46-49)

> But you will receive *power* when the Holy Spirit comes on you; and you will be my *witnesses*... (Acts 1:8)

In both of Luke's Great Commission verses above, he articulated our *call* to be witnesses as well as our *empowerment* to be witnesses! Don't miss the *clear Gospel message* Jesus provided: the simple historical facts of his death and resurrection, and what it means for us. Notice the "power from on high" that Jesus promises to provide to communicate that message!

When John recorded Jesus' sending us out as missionaries, he drew a parallel with the mission assignment that the Father had given him. He also documented the Holy Spirit's impartation to accomplish the task.

Again Jesus said, "Peace be with you! As the Father has sent me, I am sending you." And with that he breathed on them and said, "Receive the Holy Spirit." (John 20:21-22)

The thought may overwhelm us—that Jesus himself said that *he sends us* just like the *Father sent him.* Did Father empower Jesus for the task? Can we be assured that Jesus has equipped us in a like manner? Certainly so! That is what his Word has made clear to us. So, **go**, in his name, with his power and authority!

Empowered for His Purpose

While Jesus was with his disciples, he sent them on several short-term mission trips. Whenever he did so, he always imparted the authority of his name.

When Jesus had called the Twelve together, he gave them power and authority to *drive out all demons* and to cure diseases, and he sent them out to *preach the kingdom of God* and to *heal the sick.* (Luke 9:1-2, see also Matt. 10:1)

Notice the threefold purpose for which his power is given:

1. Preach the Gospel
2. Heal the sick
3. Cast out demons

We often see this trio in scriptural passages concerning Christ equipping his disciples. I wish to emphasize that Jesus sent us out to preach and to heal. When encountering demonic opposition, we have the power and authority to deal with that also, but we need not go looking for it.

Jesus has authorized us to go in his name and advance his kingdom. What is meant by "his name?" The name "Jesus" literally means, *the Lord our Savior.* When we pray in the name of Jesus we are appealing to the saving aspect of his character. When Jesus sends us out *in his name* it means that we have been afforded the backing of every aspect of God's character. God's character has the power to **save**, **heal** and **conquer**! I will introduce this threefold purpose here, and then expand these themes in the following chapters due to their importance to see our mission accomplished.

The Name of Jesus is Powerful for Salvation!

> Salvation is found in no one else, for there is no other name under heaven given to men by which we must be saved. (Acts 4:12)

I once traveled in southern India with my dear friend Pastor Vincent, his son Charlie, and a small team from the States. Vincent unexpectedly ordered our van stopped, and in a snap, hopped out and disappeared down a jungled trail. We figured he had gone into the underbrush for obvious reasons, but then it lasted an embarrassingly long time. As we readied to send Charlie out to check on him, Vincent came shuffling back in a hurry. "Okay, everybody out. Come now, it's all set."

Unbeknownst to us, Vincent had seen a sign for a school along the road, and had gone there to inquire if we might be allowed to share the Gospel. He even played the "I have a team from America" card. As we scurried down the trail, Vincent explained the situation, and before long we came to a simple school with open-walled bamboo construction and a banana-leaf thatched roof. With no time for consideration, we found ourselves standing before nearly two hundred bright-eyed, smiling children.

We took some time to introduce ourselves and answer questions, mainly about America. When our preliminaries hit a lull, Vincent looked right at me and prompted, "Okay, present the Gospel to them now."

My quick and silent prayer shot heavenward, "Jesus, what do I say? How do I share your message in a way they can relate?" *Tell them about Christmas*, came his immediate response. That was all Jesus prompted, but I instinctively knew what to do.

"Have you heard the story of when the Creator God came to the world as a baby?" And from that opening line I shared the Christmas narrative. They could all picture that little infant in the stable, surrounded by animals. "Do you know *why* this baby came to earth?" I continued, and explained how Jesus grew, and the perfect life he lived. I told them of Jesus' one purpose in coming to the world: to give his life for us as a payment for our sins. To riveted, wide eyes I detailed the somber account of the cross, and then the jubilant victory of the resurrection.

When finished, I asked if any children wanted to invite King Jesus to be their Savior and to promise to follow only him for the rest of their lives. When *all* of them raised their hands, I assumed that they had not understood. I took another run at it, clarifying the magnitude of such a decision—that to follow Jesus means to worship him alone as God. "*Now*, if you *still* want to receive Jesus, I want you to get on your knees and give your life completely to him." Their resolute response floored me, as all the children and most of their teachers fell to their knees and began to pray.

Jesus alone has the power to save; we alone have been authorized to share his saving message.

The Name of Jesus Has the Power to Heal

It is by the name of Jesus Christ of Nazareth, whom you crucified but whom God raised from the dead, that this man stands before you healed. (Acts 4:10)

On one particular mission trip, I had joined my dear friend, Pastor George, who whenever I visited his North Indian city, insisted that I preach at his church. On this Sunday, after the message the faithful followers filed out to attend further Bible instruction. Only two remained, a man and his crippled son. Pastor George implored, "Come with me Marty, let us pray for this boy."

I noticed that the boy's legs were skin on bones, featuring knees as bulbous protrusions. Apparently, the boy was able to stand on these legs, though unable to walk without assistance. Pastor George and I knelt on the floor beside the seated young man and each grabbed hold of one outstretched leg as we began to pray. We prayed in our own language, he in Hindi and I in English, inviting the resurrection power of Jesus Christ to infuse these crippled legs with strength.

Then we hoisted the young man to his feet. Still unable to take a step, we lowered him again to the floor and continued to pray. This process continued, up and down like a see-saw, each time inviting the boy to take a step, then each time lowering him to the floor again to implore Christ's power for healing.

The final time we raised him to his feet, Pastor George instructed the son to speak out in Hindi, "The Lord Jesus is healing me." The boy repeated the phrase, and then, amazingly, took a step. The father looked on bewildered as George and I smiled with delight. "That's right, son," Pastor George prodded in Hindi, "continue proclaiming that Jesus is healing you." The boy took another step, and then another as the strength of his own proclamation continued.

Soon, to our further astonishment, the boy was marching with knees lifted high to the rhythm of his own voice, "The Lord Jesus is healing *me*! The Lord Jesus is healing me!" After the appropriate celebration, Pastor George had the boy sit down one more time alongside his father. He spoke to the father and son earnestly. I didn't understand what he had been saying until the three bowed their heads. Pastor George spoke a phrase and the other two repeated it. Then another phrase, repeated by the father and son. They were praying to receive Jesus Christ as their Savior and Lord.

This Hindu father and his family had lived next door to this church for years. Sunday after Sunday he had witnessed the coming and going of happy worshipers. This particular Sunday, he had decided to see for himself what brought all the excitement and had carried his crippled son with him. This distinct morning a father and a son experienced the resurrection power of Jesus Christ: first in healing the son, and then in forgiving their sins.

We have been authorized to demonstrate the healing power of Jesus' saving message.

The Name of Jesus Has the Power to Deliver From Darkness

> For he has rescued us from the dominion of darkness and brought us into the kingdom of the Son he loves, in whom we have redemption, the forgiveness of sins. (Col. 1:13-14)

On another Sunday morning, accompanied by my friend Dan, I spoke for a church in a major South Indian city. After the message, we gave an invitation for anyone who wanted to receive prayer. We prayed for each person who came forward according to his or her need. When we began praying for a particular young woman, she was thrown to the ground with violent convulsions. "Leave us alone," demons hissed through the woman's mouth. "This one belongs to us!"

In obvious need of deliverance, Dan and I together focused our prayer attention on her. We rebuked the demons in Jesus' name, but after a considerable time of prayer, we unnervingly appeared to be making little progress.

At that point an older believer picked up a drum and began pounding it as he belted out the old spiritual, "There is power, power, wonder working power, in the blood of the Lamb; there is power, power, wonder working power, in the precious blood of the Lamb."

Just while thinking to myself, *"that's not helping…"* a demon screamed through the voice of the tormented, "Stop singing that song…I HATE THAT SONG!" which brought knowing nods from Dan and me as the rest of the faithful immediately joined the drum-led chorus in unison. Shortly thereafter, the demons left screaming, and this perplexed young lady came to herself. She eagerly embraced the Savior, now made possible by this act of deliverance.

We have been authorized to set captives free in order that they might receive the saving message of Jesus.

Jesus has authorized us to embark on a mission with him. When we join Jesus, he provides power to save, heal and conquer as we participate in an adventure in which all things are possible for those who believe.

Jesus, increase my faith. I invite you to stretch my paradigms so that they're big enough to embrace the plan and purpose you have for me. I have always known that your name has the power to save, the power to heal, and the power to deliver. Now, give me the faith to put that belief into practice. Amen.

Accomplish It!

- Consider the *authority* scriptures laid out in this chapter. What do you think about the idea that God has given you a spiritual "sheriff's badge"?

- How can you learn how to appropriate the authority you have been given?

- Begin reading the book of Acts in the Bible, chapter-by-chapter, daily asking the Holy Spirit to ignite in your own heart fresh vision for accomplishing the Great Commission.

- Exercise your kingdom-building authority by praying through the prayer guides: *30 Days of Prayer for the Muslim World, Hindu World Prayer Guide, Buddhist World Prayer Guide*, and *Pray for the 31 Frontier Peoples*. All available at https://www.worldchristian.com. Mobilize prayer groups in your church to also use these powerful resources.

Chapter 14

Empowered to Preach

If Jesus Christ be God and died for me, then no sacrifice
can be too great for me to make for Him.
— C.T. Studd

On the day of Pentecost, a fire fell from heaven that remains on Christ's followers to this day. That holy flame enabled a simple fisherman to proclaim one of the most eloquent Gospel messages recorded in Scripture. That same Spirit of God will enable *you* to share his Word with power beyond your natural capability, because it will not be you alone sharing it, but Christ living in you!

I have been crucified with Christ and I no longer live, but Christ lives in me. The life I live in the body, I live by faith in the Son of God, who loved me and gave himself for me. (Gal. 2:20)

A fisherman named Peter delivered an uncomplicated Gospel and three thousand listeners responded in faith! The clarity of his message was combined with authority from above. This straightforward Good News still has power to save through whomever it is spoken.

Always Be Ready

"But in your hearts set apart Christ as Lord. Always be prepared to give an answer to everyone who asks you to give the reason for the hope that you have. But do this with gentleness and respect." (1 Pet. 3:15)

Kelly and I were in the south Indian city of Chennai preparing for a day of ministry with Daisy, our Indian missionary friend. As we spent time in prayer, Kelly received a strong impression from the Lord that within the day, she would meet and lay hands on someone struggling with a wrenching child-loss pain. This came as a bittersweet revelation, as we ourselves had been deep in the trenches of infertility and loss for years. Admittedly, Kelly was nervously expectant, but also seasoned in faith enough to know that if God would lead her, she would obey.

The three of us set out for an afternoon of ministry in a sprawling slum, one which drew many from various regions of India in search of opportunity. The majority found utter destitution. Kelly and I felt privileged to partner with Daisy, a vivacious and winsome gal a bit younger than Kelly, who delightfully served the Lord among the poor and downtrodden. We meandered through ramshackle dwellings made mostly of clay, tin and cardboard, greeting and smiling at each person we encountered.

As we navigated one particularly muddy, filth-trodden lane, a woman grabbed onto Daisy and quite forcefully led us toward what we surmised was her home. Daisy and Kelly stooped low to duck under its earthen archway into a dank shadowy room, while I felt compelled to remain outside and intercede for this obviously divine appointment. When they finally emerged after a lengthy time—and no small amount of commotion from within—they had a crazy testimony of God's faithfulness. I'll let Kelly tell this part of the story in her own words.

As my eyes adjusted inside the chamber, I could see a small shelf on the wall opposite me where several contorted idols sat, eerily glowing by a single lit candle. The woman seemed rather proud of her disfigured collection, acting out for us, with hands pressed together and waist bowing toward them, how she worshipped and appeased them. It became clear, however, that there was also some tension between her and her gods as she thumped praying hands to her forehead, and then, with tears springing from her eyes, clenched her abdomen. She began wailing in hysterics, gesturing between the shelf and her body, back and forth, in a frenzied, exhausting dance. In more of a desperate panic than unflinching faith, I shot up a prayer for help, and as clear as a bell I sensed the Lord's voice: *Tell her I lost my son, too.*

I felt clearly that I was to share the Gospel right then and there with this grieving woman, so without wasting a minute I turned to Daisy and directed, 'Translate for me!"

I began explaining that I was a Christian—one who follows only Jesus Christ. Pointing to her shelf, I said that there are no other gods but him, and step-by-step laid out the Gospel, including telling her that God "lost" his only son too: that he gave his Son unto death on a cross as a gift of salvation for any of us to receive. The woman's frenzied tears softened and her body relaxed into gentle sobs. Daisy and I laid our hands upon her and asked if she would like to receive Jesus as her Savior, to not only bring comfort to her earthly loss, but to truly fill her with life everlasting. She said yes, and as we prayed, having her repeat and pray along with us, her countenance changed. Her anguished face smoothed and furrowed eyes brightened. Hands curled in fevered disappointment opened skyward in release and joy. We celebrated together in her squatty clay hut with mingling of words recognized and utterances unknown to me. Then the woman did the unimaginable. She reached to her shelf and threw down one of her figurines. Each one followed of her own volition, with what seemed to Daisy and me an ever-increasing glow on the woman's face. God had done it! He freed a daughter and was blessing her with new life!

When three women emerged from the dwelling to where I was waiting, they were hugging and crying. While Kelly's eyes adjusted to the brightness of the sunshine outside, she caught my look of curiosity and described the happenings within the home. We began walking away from the woman still babbling joyously from behind us, hands lifted, waving, praising.

Daisy began giggling and Kelly followed suit. She turned to Daisy and said, "I know, right? That was amazing!"

Daisy replied, "I've never done that before."

Still emotionally charged, Kelly clarified, "What, you mean lead someone to Christ?"

"Oh, no," Daisy grinned, "I mean, I don't speak that woman's language!"

A feather could have tipped us over. Mouth aghast, Kelly and I realized that in her white Western naiveté, she had assumed that because Daisy was a brown-skinned Indian, she could naturally communicate with any other dark-skinned Southeast Asian person. In her haste to share the Gospel, Kelly had counted on Daisy to interpret for her as she spoke in English, laying out the plan of salvation to a desperate soul. Imagine Daisy's wonderment as she opened her own mouth to speak a dialect *she did not know*, having faith that God Almighty *would need to speak through her* to accomplish his good purpose that day in a dank hut buried in a vast slum on the Asian subcontinent. Whoa, God! He had empowered *both* Kelly and Daisy to preach the Gospel with a downcast woman in an extraordinary way!

The Power of Preaching the Gospel

> I am not ashamed of the Gospel, because it is the power of God for the salvation of everyone who believes: first for the Jew, then for the Gentile. For in the Gospel a righteousness from God is revealed, a righteousness that is by faith from first to last, just as it is written: "The righteous will live by faith." (Rom. 1:16-17)

The power of God is embedded within the Gospel message and we have been authorized to *preach it*. I realize that the idea of *preaching* the Gospel has become unpopular with many today. They prefer the subtler approach of witnessing through actions alone, somehow regarding preaching as condemning hell-fire. No! We preach a message of utterly Good News, bringing life and reconciliation to God. We all know John 3:16 verbatim, but its two following verses further describe the saving message we are sent to speak:

> For God did not send his Son into the world to condemn the world, but to save the world through him. Whoever believes in him is not condemned, but whoever does not believe stands condemned already because he has not believed in the name of God's one and only Son. (John 3:17-18)

For people to believe, we must speak. The God who spoke the whole world into existence has likewise given us the authority to speak life into the soul of another. Yes, our message must be authenticated by a life that reflects Jesus, but the power is inherent in the Gospel and that Gospel *must be announced* to unleash its saving power.

> How, then, can they call on the one they have not believed in? And how can they believe in the one of whom they have not heard? And how can they hear without someone preaching to them? (Rom. 10:14)

We are not the source of its power. God has infused his message with saving power and calls us as the delivery agent—Kelly and Daisy were great examples of this!

> For Christ did not send me to baptize, but to preach the
> Gospel—not with words of human wisdom, lest the cross of
> Christ be emptied of its power. For the message of the cross is
> foolishness to those who are perishing, but to us who are being
> saved it is the power of God. (1 Cor. 1:17-18)

Obviously, the devil wants to dissuade us from the very action that strikes a crushing blow to his domain. Preaching the Good News of the death and resurrection of Jesus Christ liberates sinners from his tyrannical rule. Jesus preached with kingdom power on hillsides and in synagogues; Peter did so when the fire fell at Pentecost, and also preached the Good News in Cornelius' house. Paul preached with kingdom power in Athens before philosophers and in chains before King Agrippa. Friends, this is what we are called to do, from the streets of Calcutta to our favorite coffee shop among friends. Wherever we might preach the Good News, let us appropriate the power given to us to bring salvation.

Authorized to Preach

We carry with us an official "badge," the name of Jesus, authorizing us to deliver his life-giving message of salvation. This authority supersedes any government, school district or religious leadership that would declare otherwise. The original disciples presented this badge when authorities challenged them and commanded them to no longer speak in the name of Jesus.

> Then they called them in again and commanded them not to
> speak or teach at all in the name of Jesus. But Peter and John re-
> plied, "Judge for yourselves whether it is right in God's sight to
> obey you rather than God. For we cannot help speaking about
> what we have seen and heard." (Acts 4:18-20)

This God-given authority grants us the right and the obligation to speak in the name of Jesus. We must not fear the world's intimidation, intent on silencing our voice and our message.

When Kelly and I served in Turkey, it was illegal to share the Gospel in public or to distribute Christian literature. For weeks, we simply served victims devastated by a flash flood, which had taken over one hundred lives in a single neighborhood. God sent us to not only mend houses, but also broken hearts. We did not interact with the local imam

(Muslim cleric), but he had obviously been observing us all the while. I recall frustration at our limited opportunity to proclaim the Gospel. Yes, we were ministering tangibly, and the Lord opened a few doors for us to lay hands on the sick and see him bring about some remarkable healings. But I agitatedly wondered when we would have opportunity to proclaim the name of our Savior Jesus and explain that his love was our motivation for serving.

After a month of manually demonstrating the love of God, our team felt a release from Father to speak his saving message of love. On the busiest market day of the week we were compelled to set up in the city's center square, where throngs of people bustled about at the height of the Muslim observance of Ramadan. Our team began to present the Gospel in a drama set to music. Afterward, I stood up front, and with a portable PA system addressed more than a thousand onlookers who pressed in to see and hear what the commotion was all about. I shared the way to reconciliation with God through Messiah Jesus.

Yes, we were breaking man's law, and we could certainly have been imprisoned, deported or even worse. Yet we continued publicly in the crowded market, proclaiming the powerful message of hope. Upon con-clusion of our Gospel presentation, the local imam—who had the most vested interest to call authorities and have us arrested—pleaded with us to allow him to personally escort us into his mosque. With our entire team secluded in a private area of the looming building, he introduced us to his wife. Then he asked us to lay hands on her and to pray that Jesus would heal her womb and bless them with a child. Extraordinary! We never heard the outcome of our prayers, but I believe that Jesus responded and blessed this precious cleric and his wife with offspring. We have since occasionally prayed for them and earnestly hope that they eventually found new life in Jesus.

The following day one of the families that we had served by repair-ing their flood-damaged home invited us to come back one last time as their honored guests. The family knew that we were soon returning to America and wanted to bless us with hospitality and a big party to thank us for all we had done. They invited the entire neighborhood and we delighted in the apple tea, goat cheese, fresh bread and pastries that they prepared for all present. We determined that we would have a farewell gift for them also, presented in the form of a dramatic performance and short message.

Near the conclusion of the party we acted out our "gift" and everyone gathered around with wide-eyed amazement to watch the drama. As all began to hear our message, approaching sirens blared from down the street. Two police cars arrived in a cloud of dust and concern covered faces all around us. We froze, unsure what to do, but the adult son of the family hosting the party approached the policemen, and with bewildering boldness prepared to defend us. The officers stepped from their cars and the young man spoke forcefully, "What are you doing here? Leave these people alone. They are our friends and our honored guests. Allow us to show them the respect that they deserve." We could not believe our eyes as we watched the Turkish policemen step back into their cars and slowly drive away. Father wanted his children to finish hearing the message of love and reconciliation through his Son Jesus.

I realize that events do not always unfold this way. Sometimes a great price must be paid for the privilege of sharing the Gospel, as the original disciples were well aware. It is imperative to listen and respond to the promptings of Jesus rather than stepping out in presumption. Had I impatiently stepped out and proclaimed the Gospel weeks beforehand as I had wanted to do, a different and perhaps adverse outcome may have resulted.

Advancing His Kingdom of Light

Jesus has brought us his darkness-shattering, liberating message of truth, and the authority to speak it boldly. Through his death and resurrection, Jesus defeated sin, death, and the power of the devil. His victory over sin empowers us to preach. His victory over death empowers us to heal. His victory over the devil empowers us to conquer.

Because Jesus defeated sin, we can preach forgiveness in his name and bring restored relationships with the Father to all who will receive it. Yet the life-giving effect of the Good News does not stop there. Jesus has also defeated death and the devil, and we must learn to practically apply those victories.

The word "kingdom" simply means where a king reigns, or the domain of a king. Jesus is the King of kings and the Lord of lords, who rules and reigns over all the earth. Yet he has given us—royal sons and daughters of God—the right, responsibility and authority to take dominion over what is rightfully his. If God's children do not exercise that dominion, then the devil will continue to rule as if he is the king. Like the chief and his tribe in Equatorial Guinea, the people will continue to sit under the dark rule of this evil dictator.

We are charged to shine God's light by preaching the Gospel. We are literally his vessels of spiritual light, called to advance his kingdom reign in a land enshrouded by darkness.

> For we do not preach ourselves, but Jesus Christ as Lord, and ourselves as your servants for Jesus' sake. For God, who said, "Let light shine out of darkness," made his light shine in our hearts to give us the light of the knowledge of the glory of God in the face of Christ. But we have this treasure in jars of clay to show that this all-surpassing power is from God and not from us. (2 Cor. 4:5-7)

When we share the Gospel, we displace darkness with the light of God's indwelling. Although we are merely jars of clay, we are vessels carrying *his* light. This purpose is a reflection of Christ himself. Jesus fulfilled the following word written about himself by Isaiah and recorded by Matthew:

> ". . .the people living in darkness have seen a great light; on those living in the land of the shadow of death a light has dawned." From that time on Jesus began to preach, "Repent, for the kingdom of heaven is near." (Matt. 4:16-17)

Jesus has called you and me as his light to dispel darkness.

> "You are the light of the world. A city on a hill cannot be hidden. Neither do people light a lamp and put it under a bowl. Instead they put it on its stand, and it gives light to everyone in the house. In the same way, let your light shine before men, that they may see your good deeds and praise your Father in heaven. . ." (Matt. 5:14-16)

God calls us to preach his kingdom-advancing message until all have heard of King Jesus. As we will encounter in the next chapter, this King stands ready to confirm his message through signs and wonders that accompany it.

Jesus, I confess that at times I have been more like a lamp under a bowl than a bright city on a hill. Forgive me for the times I have been ashamed of the

Gospel. I recognize that it is the enemy that wants to sow fear in my heart and rob the joy of seeing others come to new life in you. I bind fear in Jesus' name and pray for new courage to shine for you through my actions and my words. Amen.

Accomplish It!

- How does the Holy Spirit empower us to share the Gospel message?

- What are the kingdom-building implications of the indwelling of the Holy Spirit?

- How does preaching the Gospel advance the kingdom of light? How have you personally witnessed this truth in action?

- What could you do to better prepare yourself to share the Gospel with others?

- Order and learn to use the Evangecube as a simple tool and method for witnessing (http://www.e3resources.org).

Chapter 15

Empowered to Heal

There is nothing impossible with God. All the impossibility is with us when we measure God by the limitations of our unbelief.
— Smith Wigglesworth

My Indian friend Vincent announced his grand agenda for our weekend together. "Brother Marty," he began, "I am so excited to see what Jesus will do when we go down to the village of Pudukkottai this weekend. The Lord has put this place on my heart and I believe that this is the time for us to plant a church there. This is what we will do. I have made arrangements to book the town hall and we will advertise a big event. Brother Dan will give a concert and you will share the Gospel. I have prepared young Franklin as a pastor, so whoever comes to the Lord that evening, Franklin will stay behind and care for the new believers. So we will plant a church this weekend. How does that sound to you, brother?"

Vincent's plan sounded audacious to me, perhaps even overly optimistic, but I wasn't about to say that to my elder host, so I simply agreed, "It sounds wonderful, brother Vincent!" My pastor friend, however, failed to mention the required seventeen-hour, bone-jarring bus ride through the night. Nor that seemingly every five minutes during the excursion we would face certain death from a head-on collision with a dilapidated lorry (a large Indian cargo truck). Either our bus, or an oncoming lorry would repeatedly attempt overtaking another vehicle and only at the very last possible second would swerve back into its own lane. We only had several minutes to be thankful we were still alive before bracing again to meet our Maker in another near-death experience.

Dan, Wayne and I unloaded in Pudukkottai, completely frazzled, as our Indian brothers, Franklin, Vincent and his son Charlie, seemed oddly rested and ready to go. With little time to recover, Vincent soon had us hitting the streets, pumping out handbills to promote our concert the following evening.

When the heat of that afternoon became unbearable, we retreated to the home where we were lodging. While taking rest, something seemed dramatically wrong with Dan. His breathing became labored. He said he felt dizzy, so he lay down on the cool stone floor. His condition continued to deteriorate literally by the minute. Then, quite swiftly, Dan became unresponsive. The dark shroud of impending death seemed to hover like a thick blanket around us. Dan was completely unconscious as Wayne and I frantically checked for a pulse. His labored, shallow breathing diminished, and then vanished. I desperately looked for any sign of life but found none. In that moment I had an incapacitating visualization, that of calling Dan's wife, Chris, to inform her that her husband was dead. Fear knocked the wind out of me, and I fought to suck air back into my own lungs. I considered administering CPR on Dan, but instinctively called for everyone to pray instead. Wayne, Charlie, and I went to our knees around Dan's motionless frame and began to cry out to God. Faith welled up inside me as I rebuked the devourer.

"You cannot take him, Satan. Dan belongs to the Most High God. We rebuke the spirit of death in Jesus' name and claim the resurrection power of the living God to restore our brother to life and perfect health. Jesus, we need you." My petition came strong and unabated. Faith had found its footing, and within the gravity of the situation, I was expressing it.

As we prayed over Dan together—he would recount this to us later—he watched the scene unfold from an overhead perspective. Dan could see his frame lying on the floor, and he watched as we knelt around him to petition God and confront the enemy. At the point when we had claimed the resurrection power of Jesus, his third-person perspective changed and he opened his eyes, encountering our joyful, tear-stained faces looking back at him.

Everything transpired so quickly that we were unsure what had actually happened. When Dan opened his eyes and sat up, I threw my arms around him and our petitions to God turned to joyful praises. "I thought we had lost you, buddy," I choked, muscling a big squeeze. It was obvious that the devil did not want us in Pudukkottai sharing the Gospel and was prepared to do anything to oppose us.[47]

Power for the Battle

When advancing God's kingdom, we must realize that we are engaged in a battle for lost souls and the enemy will not give them up without a fight. Satan wanted to take Dan out of commission because Dan was a key to God's plan to establish his church. Thankfully, we do not have to contend with the devil in our own strength. When Jesus sends out his followers on a mission-driven assignment, he also provides the power and authority to achieve the task. So, as we go, we are authorized to preach, heal, and conquer.

> When Jesus had called the Twelve together, he gave them power and authority to drive out all demons and to cure diseases, and he sent them out to preach the kingdom of God and to heal the sick. (Luke 9:1-2)

In Mark's Great Commission account, he made it clear that signs and wonders are part of Jesus' mission program.

> He said to them, "Go into all the world and preach the Good News to all creation. Whoever believes and is baptized will be saved, but whoever does not believe will be condemned. And these signs will accompany those who believe: In my name they will drive out demons; they will speak in new tongues; they will pick up snakes with their hands; and when they drink deadly poison, it will not hurt them at all; they will place their hands on sick people, and they will get well." (Mark 16:15-18)

Unsurprisingly, Mark goes on to report such events happening just as predicted. So why should it surprise us then when the miraculous happens in *our* Gospel-sharing? You may even wonder why healing needs to take an important role in Christ's kingdom-expanding strategy.

Victory Over Sin and Death

Remember that sickness infiltrated the world through sin. Jesus, through the cross and resurrection, defeated sin, death, and the powerful bondage of the enemy. The Good News of Jesus is not merely a distant future promise of heaven, but a kingdom-building, darkness-shattering reality here and now!

Many of us have a practical understanding that Jesus defeated sin, so therefore provides forgiveness. Father no longer holds my sin against me, and thus I no longer need to be eternally separated from him, but instead I can anticipate abundant life in a restored relationship with the Father. This is great news that must be announced to the whole world.

But we must further have a practical understanding of the implications of Jesus' victory over death. The fall of Adam and Eve brought death into the world.

> And the LORD God commanded the man, "You are free to eat from any tree in the garden; but you must not eat from the tree of the knowledge of good and evil, for when you eat of it you will surely die." (Gen. 2:16-17)

With this original "death" came sickness and disease. Ironically, the final defeat of death comes through death—the death when Jesus breathed his last on the cross as the devil and his demons squealed with delight. But you and I know that this is not how the story ends! Jesus had predicted these events to his disciples, describing plainly what would happen next.

> We are going up to Jerusalem, and the Son of Man will be betrayed to the chief priests and the teachers of the law. They will condemn him to death and will turn him over to the Gentiles to be mocked and flogged and crucified. On the third day he will be raised to life! (Matt. 20:18-19)

Through Christ's death, death was defeated. Jesus rose from the dead to live forever. We have been given promise of the same!

> Or don't you know that all of us who were baptized into Christ Jesus were baptized into his death? We were therefore buried with him through baptism into death in order that, just as Christ was raised from the dead through the glory of the Father, we too may live a new life. If we have been united with him like this in his death, we will certainly also be united with him in his resurrection. (Rom. 6:3-5)

The Message-Confirming Power of God

Jesus calls us to heal the sick and raise the dead to demonstrate the reality of his kingdom here and now. While on earth, Jesus healed many sick individuals and even raised Lazarus, the widow's son, and the ruler's daughter from death. We may wonder about the purpose, since healed individuals certainly encountered sickness at some point again, and even those miraculously brought back to life eventually physically died. Jesus was authenticating his message through these miraculous works and he promises to do the same through us!

> Believe me when I say that I am in the Father and the Father is in me; or at least believe on the evidence of the miracles themselves. I tell you the truth, anyone who has faith in me will do what I have been doing. He will do even greater things than these, because I am going to the Father. And I will do whatever you ask in my name, so that the Son may bring glory to the Father. You may ask me for anything in my name, and I will do it. (John 14:11-14)

Jesus sends us out both with his message and his power to authenticate it.

Our small band of Indian and American brothers gathered at the town hall early in our second evening in Pudukkottai. As we joined hands in prayer we were especially thankful for restoring our brother Dan to full vitality. We invited the presence of Jesus to fill that meeting place and asked him to draw souls to himself as we gave glory to God. We were surprised to see a swarm of people assemble in the conference hall long before the event was scheduled to begin. By the time Dan started playing his guitar, an entirely Hindu crowd had packed the venue. Dan was incredibly gifted to draw hearts in as he sang and played. He even motivated the audience to join in on choruses proclaiming Jesus as Lord, even though most did not understand what they were singing about! I felt deep anticipation when it was my turn to preach the message.

I tried to keep it as simple as possible, describing God as the Creator of the universe who formed us in his image because of his desire to have children. Vincent translated for me as I explained how all of us had broken our relationship with God by siding with Satan and believing his lies. I shared the ultimate sacrifice the Father made when he gave up his own Son to take the penalty for the punishment we deserved because of our sins. I saw awe on their faces as I explained how Jesus rose victoriously from the grave and offers us forgiveness, new life, and redemption as children of God. I made it clear that to follow Jesus we must follow him alone, forsaking all other gods. Then I invited individuals to come forward if they wanted prayer to have their sins washed away and to become followers of Jesus.

I had to conceal my disappointment when absolutely no one responded—nor even moved—as if they were waiting for something else to happen. During the long silence that followed, I asked Jesus, "What do we do now?"

He prompted, *Invite the sick to come forward to receive prayer in my name. My presence is here and I will heal them.*

I was initially taken aback by this. I had never given this kind of invitation before. In my heart I debated, *How dare I invite Hindus to come forward to be healed by Jesus?* While I was still wrestling with the Lord, Dan came over and whispered in my ear. "Marty, I can feel the presence of God in this place. I believe Jesus wants us to pray for the sick, and that he will heal them."

My heart was pounding, but I could argue with the Lord no more. It was clear what he wanted and Dan confirmed it. "The presence of God is here in this place," I announced. "If anyone is sick, we will pray for you in the name of Jesus, and Jesus will heal you." Even as the words spilled out of my mouth, I could not believe what I was saying. But as soon as I offered the invitation, men and women began to stream forward, crowding the front. Each of us quickly paired up with a native-speaking partner and, though unrehearsed, we all began to pray in like manner. We would ask each person, "What do you want Jesus to do for you?" They would respond by describing an ailment. Then we would pray specifically for Jesus' healing to come, and finally, through our translators, we would ask if they could feel any change.

I remember a doctor who came forward and pronounced to me in perfect English, "I would like to ask Jesus to heal my right ear. I have lost all hearing. Please pray for me."

As Charlie and I placed our hands on the doctor's ear, I said a simple prayer: "Jesus, touch this man's ear. In your name, Jesus, we ask that it would be completely healed. Amen."

The man turned his head from side to side. I asked, "How is it now? Can you hear from your right ear?"

"Oh yes, I can hear perfectly now," he responded as he continued to turn his head side to side, listening from each ear in turn. "Both ears are fine now. Thank you very much for praying for me in the name of Jesus."

While still talking to this man, I heard screaming from the other side of the room. Dan and Vincent had been petitioning the Lord for a woman to regain her sight. Dan later explained that the eyes of the elderly woman were glossy white when she came forward asking for prayer. "I want to see again," was her simple request. Dan and Vincent placed their hands over the woman's eyes and prayed in the name of Jesus for healing. When they took their hands away, Dan saw something like scales fall to the ground, revealing clear, deep brown eyes. That was when she started screaming. In her native tongue she was shrieking, "I can see! I can see!"

It was nearly an hour later when we finished praying for the last person who had come forward. No one had left the hall, and every person who had requested prayer had been healed. I felt the Shepherd nudging me to repeat my invitation to become followers of Jesus. It was then that the greatest miracle of the evening occurred. Immediately a dozen hearts were opened to receive new life. Vincent gathered them into a circle to invite Jesus into their lives. It was a holy moment.

Something profound then took place as Vincent introduced this small group of new believers to Franklin. "I want you all to meet your new pastor, Franklin. He will teach you how to be followers of Jesus." Franklin made his way around the interior of the circle, looking into the eyes of each person as he greeted them and learned their names. That very evening, Jesus planted a new church that would soon grow and bring about much fruit.[48]

As the evening was brought to conclusion our hearts overflowed with joy and I was reminded of a simple promise of Jesus, "…I will build my church, and the gates of Hades will not overcome it." (Matt. 16:18b) Jesus did it that night in Pudukkottai and the enemy was powerless to stop it!

Likewise, Jesus planted a church in Corinth through Paul, the sent one. In the apostle's letter to that young church he reminded them that their faith was not founded on him, but on the Lord.

> My message and my preaching were not with wise and persuasive words, but with a demonstration of the Spirit's power, so that your faith might not rest on men's wisdom, but on God's power. (1 Cor. 2:4-5)

Brothers and sisters, God has empowered us to preach and to heal. We must also believe that with this same authority we confront our enemy.

Jesus, I admit that I feel a little like the man who confessed, "Lord, I believe, help me overcome my unbelief." I believe that your Word is true and your promises are unchanging. Yet I struggle with the discrepancy between what I read in the Bible and what I see demonstrated in my own life. Lord, I accept your Word at face value and ask for the faith to put your Word into practice. Use me as your vessel to bring hope and healing to the lost. Make me unafraid to battle my enemy. Amen.

Accomplish It!

- Consider the scriptures provided in this chapter about the followers of Jesus being empowered to heal. Have you seen this reality demonstrated through your own life or others close to you?

- How does healing demonstrate Christ's victory over sin?

- What did Jesus say about miraculous signs validating the message we are sent to preach?

- This authority is not only available to frontline missionaries. Look for opportunities this week to pray for people who are suffering from various illnesses. Make it a habit to ask, "Can I pray for you now and invite Jesus to heal you?"

Chapter 16

Empowered to Defeat the Enemy

The first step on the way to victory is to recognize the enemy.
— Corrie ten Boom

Though excited about my upcoming trip to India, to be honest I had no idea what to expect. My friend Gideon, from Bangalore, had invited me to travel with him, visiting churches he had planted in the east-central Indian states of Orissa and Chhattisgarh. I knew from experience that I would be expected to guest-speak at churches and programs so I sought God earnestly for messages to bring. His response was clear, yet troubling, *You do not need to prepare anything, I will give you my specific message for each place you visit.* I remembered Jesus' words in Mark 13:11, "…do not worry beforehand about what to say. Just say whatever is given you at the time, for it is not you speaking, but the Holy Spirit."

Okay, Lord, I'm not sure where I'm going or what I will say—that sounds like an adventure! And it was.

Gideon met me at the airport in the city of Raipur and the next day we headed for the hills in a hired Jeep. He announced his big plan for our day: "Brother, tomorrow morning is Sunday and I have arranged for you to speak in five house churches. We will have to get up very early because it is a one-hour drive to the first church and about an hour drive between each of the other churches. So, we will only have about an hour and a half at each church. The brothers and sisters are very excited to meet you and hear the Word of the Lord that you have brought for them." *No pressure, right?*

Bumping along gravel roads, Gideon and I looked out from the back seat as the awaited sun rose to reveal green rolling landscape. I had been praying since we climbed into the Jeep, *"Father, what do you want me to say to your children. I ask you to give me a word from your heart to your people."* It was not until halfway to my first assignment that a single Bible reference finally dropped into my mind. I pulled my well-worn travel Bible from my backpack and opened to that scripture. I recognized the text and my handwritten notes in the margin, and knew exactly what to say. This Spirit-prompted program continued throughout the day. A specific scripture joined to a specific message, for each church we visited. By early afternoon we neared the third house church on Gideon's itinerary when Holy Spirit highlighted for me 1 Corinthians 6:19, 'Do you not know that your body is a temple of the Holy Spirit, who is in you, whom you have received from God? You are not your own; you were bought at a price. Therefore honor God with your body." While still reflecting on the implications of that passage, Gideon began to usher me out of our trusty, now dust-covered rig and into a packed home, lit up with smiling faces ready to greet me.

After several enthusiastic worship songs that I did not understand, but clapped along with anyway, Gideon introduced me and proceeded to translate as I carefully articulated the selected text. I had barely begun to speak about this profound mystery of the Holy Spirit of God dwelling within us, when a blood-curdling cry arose from among those seated on woven floor mats. The young woman twisted and convulsed in such a violent commotion that five men promptly attempted to restrain her. In that very moment, Gideon looked straight at me and said, "Brother Marty, please, go and cast out the demon." Although the five men seemed no match for the present strength of this 110-pound woman, I approached in an attempt to respond to Gideon's request. As I neared the woman she thrashed violently and one of her rings cut my left arm, which instantly began to bleed. Darting evil eyes caught sight of the dripping red fluid and she promptly tried to lick it up, causing me to instinctively pull my arm away. "In the name of Jesus, I command you to be still!" I demanded, to little effect. "Demon, I rebuke you in Jesus' name and demand that you release this woman." Some amount of thrashing subsided but the demonic presence was not yielding. The evil entity within her caused this woman to appear hideously deformed and twisted. Gideon came alongside me, adding his rebuke, "You are a rebellious and belligerent spirit and we demand that you come out of this woman now in Jesus' name." Still no release.

In past conflicts with demonic entities, I had always witnessed the Lord's victory, but had also seen the process take over an hour. I sensed that on this occasion such delay was its sinister objective. The enemy did not want God's people to receive his appointed word and was prepared for a disruptive holdout. With this in mind, I confronted the evil presence one last time saying, "You are in disobedience to King Jesus. I have commanded you to come out in his name and by his authority. King Jesus will hold you accountable for every minute that you remain in continued disobedience to his authority." With that, I motioned to the five men to escort the woman, by this time slightly easier to restrain, into the next room that so that she would no longer be a distraction.

Based on the direction I felt from the Lord, I continued my message.

There is a place within each of our hearts that is reserved for God. Father longs to dwell in each one of us by the presence of the Holy Spirit. As it says in 2 Cor. 4:6-10, "For God, who said, 'Let light shine out of darkness,' made his light shine in our hearts to give us the light of the knowledge of the glory of God in the face of Christ. But we have this treasure in jars of clay to show that this all-surpassing power is from God and not from us. We are hard pressed on every side, but not crushed; perplexed, but not in despair; persecuted, but not abandoned; struck down, but not destroyed. We always carry around in our body the death of Jesus, so that the life of Jesus may also be revealed in our body."

We have witnessed today that the devil tries to inhabit places that rightfully belong to God. The devil is a squatter that possesses places that don't belong to him. The enemy must be evicted from every corner of our hearts so that we become completely consecrated to Jesus and shine as vessels of light for his glory.

When I had finished the message, we spent time in fervent prayer, consecrating our hearts to King Jesus only. The service concluded and it would soon be time to continue to our next appointed stop. Gideon approached me with the tormented woman following after him, "Marty," Gideon said, "the demon came and told me, 'have that man pray again and I will go.' I told it that it was a lying spirit, but it pleaded all the more asking that you command it to go one last time. What do you think we should do?"

"Let's command it to go, one more time together, Gideon. I think it's afraid to continue in its disobedience to Jesus." And so, together, Gideon and I appealed to our authority in the name of Jesus and commanded that the demon be cast out of this woman, never to return! Immediately a shriek shot out and the woman dropped to the floor completely lifeless.

Within a few moments, she began to move and arose as if waking from a bad dream. An unmistakable transformation emerged before our very eyes. The woman, previously ugly, vile, twisted, now stood in front of us erect, calm, radiant. She appeared like royalty in her bright blue sari with silver embroidery. Never had I seen such a complete metamorphosis of a person's countenance. This young woman now readily confessed Jesus Christ as her Lord and Savior and both Gideon and I felt that she should be baptized right on the spot. In the home was a sizable clay vessel filled with water, much like ones I pictured Jesus using at the wedding feast in Canaan when he turned water into wine. We poured the entire contents of the vessel over this transformed, living vessel before us. She welcomed the water, soaking and smiling beautifully in her brilliant blue sari. She was the sparkling image of a temple of the Holy Spirit!

Two Kingdoms in Conflict

Some might ask skeptically, "What exactly is going on here? What's this business of casting out demons? Is that even real?" The answer begins quite fundamentally: there exist both physical and spiritual realms. Between these two realms exists a cause and effect relationship. Furthermore, the kingdom of light and kingdom of darkness oppose one other among both physical and spiritual domains.

> For he has rescued us from the dominion of darkness and
> brought us into the kingdom of the Son he loves, in whom we
> have redemption, the forgiveness of sins. (Col. 1:13-14)

The royal children of God have received divine authority to take dominion by advancing the kingdom of God. When we respond in obedience by functioning in the power of Holy Spirit to preach, heal, and conquer, the kingdom of God is expanded, and the kingdom of darkness is diminished. The enemy holds in bondage those who rightfully belong to the Father until the children of God set them free. When we march in obedience to King Jesus, captives are unshackled and released.

Ultimately Jesus will return and execute his final judgment. He will call upon one single angel to cast the ancient serpent Satan into the lake of fire.[49] But until that day, we are engaged in an eminently real spiritual battle. Our actions produce tangible consequences related to that battle. Paul gave specific instructions for engaging this spiritual warfare:

> Finally, be strong in the Lord and in his mighty power. Put on the full armor of God so that you can take your stand against the devil's schemes. For our struggle is not against flesh and blood, but against the rulers, against the authorities, against the powers of this dark world and against the spiritual forces of evil in the heavenly realms. Therefore put on the full armor of God, so that when the day of evil comes, you may be able to stand your ground, and after you have done everything, to stand. Stand firm then, with the belt of truth buckled around your waist, with the breastplate of righteousness in place, and with your feet fitted with the readiness that comes from the gospel of peace. In addition to all this, take up the shield of faith, with which you can extinguish all the flaming arrows of the evil one. Take the helmet of salvation and the sword of the Spirit, which is the word of God. And pray in the Spirit on all occasions with all kinds of prayers and requests. With this in mind, be alert and always keep on praying for all the saints. (Eph. 6:10-18)

These words are not hypothetical or merely metaphorical; they are marching orders for the precise conflict in which we are engaged. Notice from the scripture above that the enemy has organized his troops according to a military strategy, with ranking rulers, authorities, powers, and evil spiritual forces all deployed with specific assignments. We, therefore, must counter strategically to employ *our* resources, of time, money, workers, and prayer wherever he still holds territory among unreached and unengaged peoples!

Called to Advance!

We are commissioned to go and have been given a badge of authority to join this holy quest toward salvation in all the earth. We are to effect the establishment of his good kingdom, necessarily evicting Lucifer and his squatting hosts from what is not rightfully theirs!

Is Christ's victory over the devil demonstrated through our lives today? Jesus has authorized us to preach the Gospel, heal the sick, and cast out demons. When we do so, we are a living example of Christ the victor! Satan holds no territory on earth that we are not authorized to repossess. The enemy must be evicted!

Why do you suppose the Bible recounts all those graphic battles over the conquest of the Promised Land? Could it be to admonish us that our mission is to expand and take back God's kingdom on earth? Taking territory for King Jesus requires spiritual warfare. This is a lesson he is still teaching us today.

> These are the nations the LORD left to test all those Israelites who had not experienced any of the wars in Canaan (he did this only to teach warfare to the descendants of the Israelites who had not had previous battle experience). (Judg. 3:1-2)

We are embroiled in battle, whether we acknowledge it or not. We had better learn to fight! Our first arsenal is prayer, as Jesus instructed in the most famous petition ever recorded!

> Our Father in heaven, hallowed be your name, your kingdom come, your will be done on earth as it is in heaven. (Matt. 6:9b-10)

It is the will of the Father for his kingdom to be established here and now, and he has authorized us to carry out that mission. As recorded in Scripture, Jesus provides authority and then his followers go out and enforce it.

> Jesus said, "From the days of John the Baptist until now, the kingdom of heaven has been forcefully advancing, and forceful men lay hold of it." (Matt. 11:12)

In Mark 6:8-11 Jesus provided kingdom-advancing instruction. In the following verses, we read how his directives were carried out.

> They went out and *preached* that people should repent. They drove out many demons and anointed many sick people with oil and healed them. (Mark 6:12-13)

In Luke 10:1 we read that Jesus prepared a short-term mission team of seventy-two. We might wonder where these followers came from. Naturally they had multiplied. Only one chapter earlier (Luke 9:1-6) Jesus had sent out twelve disciples two-by-two. Suppose if each of those six pairs followed Jesus' example of equipping twelve more disciples, then the result would produce seventy-two disciples! At any rate, the first sixteen verses of Luke chapter 10 are dedicated to Jesus' instructions to advance his kingdom. He directs his mission team clearly: "Heal the sick who are there and tell them, 'The kingdom of God is near you.'" (Luke 10:8)

In the passage that follows we discover that the seventy-two came back with a praise report!

> The seventy-two returned with joy and said, "Lord, even the demons submit to us in your name." (Luke 10:17)

Of course that's what happened, because Jesus gave them authority, commissioned and sent them, and they went out in obedience. Likewise, Jesus has sent us with authorization and the only question remains: *Will we go?*

The Devil's Agenda

Make no mistake. If we refuse to go, the evil dictator will remain and exercise his terrible rule over souls kept in bondage. Jesus makes the devil's agenda painfully clear in contrast to his own.

> The *thief* comes only to steal and kill and destroy; *I* have come that they may have life, and have it to the full. (John 10:10)

Satan's agenda is clear. Kill. Steal. Destroy. Those under his control are all too familiar with the horrific effects of his rule. They are like those being led to gas chambers until the Allied armies of God's sons and daughters storm in to rescue and bring about liberty for the captives.

You may recall my friends Marlien and Miguel from chapter 5. While with Marlien in Equatorial Guinea she told me this disturbing story.

Marlien had taken a team of young evangelists on an outreach in Mbini, a small town lying at the mouth of the Benito River. They soon discovered that this beautiful coastal habitation lay under the rule of dark spirits. The team arrived and immediately began sharing the Good News of Jesus, visiting each and every home. Within days, the entire team became terribly sick. Those who were able to do so continued valiantly making house visits and sharing the Gospel.

Marlien and a few others encountered one particular home that, upon entry, felt covered in a dark blanket of sadness. They found a grief-stricken woman inside so they began to share the story of Jesus with her. They spoke of a loving God who willingly sent his only son, Jesus, to die on a cross as the sacrifice for sin; and that Jesus is the Lamb of God who paid the price once, for all.

The team could identify in the woman's eyes that she understood the message and believed it as true. But instead of becoming happy, she started to cry and grow angry. "Why have you only come now?" the woman demanded. "Why didn't you come sooner to tell me this? I just offered my second child as a sacrifice to Satan. Only now I hear that Jesus was the final sacrifice—for me—and for my family?" At that, she broke down with inconsolable sobbing. Marlien led the team first in repentance for taking so long to come to her town, after which they prayed for the woman. Asking for healing for her broken heart, they graciously extended to her forgiveness for all her sins, including the sin of offering her own children to the enemy.

The Gospel message does not only give life to an individual; it also breaks the bondage of death. Its power can set an entire people group free from the grip of Satan.

Jesus Came to Set the Captives Free

In the state of Meghalaya, India, I worked with my friend, Jonathan, at his mission training center in the northeast. Jonathan had a vision to train and send northeastern Indian believers to reach similar people groups in completely unreached areas. Jonathan introduced me to Ramesh, a young zealous national, who sought out a very remote area in the secluded, mysterious state of Arunachal Pradesh, to reach the tiny tribe known as the Monpa people group. The Monpa, numbering only a few thousand, was entirely Buddhist without a single known believer.

Moved by Ramesh's vision and zeal, I committed to pray daily for him and salvation for the Monpa tribe. I did so every day for the following three years and thus eagerly awaited his progress reports. Within a year Ramesh had assembled a small team and within another six months, Ramesh and his crew had relocated among the Monpa, in a city near the India-Bhutan border. Plans progressed well until they came under fierce spiritual attack.

When darkness fell over the city, demons would speak audibly to Ramesh and his team in their apartment. "Leave this place immediately or we will kill you. The Monpa people belong to us. We know why

you are here. We control this territory. You will leave or you will die."
Although evil voices returned night after night, Ramesh and his fellow
evangelists resolved to stay. Several months later, however, Ramesh and
several of the team fell ill and required hospitalization. Ultimately, they
all retreated to their hometowns for medical care and rest. They recovered, but did not return to the Monpa people. Though discouraged to
hear this report, I did not stop praying for God to rescue the Monpa.

Another year passed when I again visited Jonathan in northeast
India, teaching for one of his Bible schools. One afternoon, while walking with Jonathan by a guest room, I noticed a very fit, slender elderly
man and his wife. When I inquired of Jonathan, he smiled, "Oh, that's
Zima, he's the real deal." That introduction piqued my curiosity, inviting
Jonathan to continue. "Oh yeah, that guy is an evangelistic machine. He
will go into the hardest, most restricted areas and preach the Gospel
until he gets put into prison. Then his wife prays him out of prison and
they move on to preach in the next place. He's just getting back and
recovering from his last tour before he goes back out again."

"Can I meet him?"

"Sure, let's see if he's willing to have visitors now," Jonathan offered.

Moments later introductions were made, tea was poured, and I was
listening to Zima's evangelistic exploits in the far reaches of Arunachal
Pradesh. He explained how his wife prays him out of prison, as if that
is a normal thing, and told us where they went after his latest release.
When he began to describe the area, I had to interrupt to ask, "Zima, can
you tell me which people group lives there—where you recently were
sharing the Gospel?"

"Oh, yes, it is a very small people group known as the Monpa."

I nearly fell off my chair and then he nearly fell off his when I told
him that I had been praying for that tribe every day for the past three
years! We both grew so animated that we could hardly communicate.
He continued his story with a fresh zeal fanned by my own interest. He
described a small Monpa village that didn't fit the description of the city
where Ramesh and his team had once lived.

He had informed the village elders of a message so important that
the entire community must hear it. They reluctantly agreed, and the next
day Zima presented the Gospel while his wife stood on guard the entire
time, praying. Something must have broken loose in the heavenly realm,
because nearly fifty Monpa villagers committed to following Jesus. Zima

and his wife only had days to disciple this group of new believers before elders forced them to leave—threatening his very life.

"Fifty Monpa believers?" I clarified.

"Yes, about fifty. Praise the Lord. They are no longer under the bondage of Satan. They have a good King now."

We prayed and praised God together for reaching this precious people group and rescuing a remnant into the kingdom of light.

Jehovah Sneaky

Jeremiah, a missionary friend, playfully calls Jesus, "Jehovah Sneaky." The title may sound irreverent, but bear with me...the following scripture is a case in point. Notice that Jesus told his disciples to pray that workers would be sent into the harvest field, and then immediately sent *them*!

> Then he said to his disciples, "The harvest is plentiful but the workers are few. Ask the Lord of the harvest, therefore, to send out workers into his harvest field." He called his twelve disciples to him and gave them authority to drive out evil spirits and to heal every disease and sickness. (Matt. 9:37-10:1)

The disciples could have rightly protested: "Wait a minute, Jesus, we were just praying for *someone else* to go! But before we knew what happened, *we* were the ones out preaching the Gospel and casting out demons. What just happened?" Like the disciples, when we pray dangerous prayers we are likely to be sent on dangerous missions. One barely has time to ask, *How did I get signed up for this? Was I just the answer to my own prayer?* You are sneaky, God!

I've often experienced the irony of being the answer to my own prayer. Don't get me wrong: I love the results of getting "roped in" and, in hindsight, wouldn't have wanted anything else. But please understand, I'm just an ordinary guy. I never thought I would be the one preaching the Gospel, healing the sick and casting out demons! At one time I wasn't even sure if I believed in miracles or demons—my church background certainly didn't prepare me for this. Never in my wildest dreams had I imagined that God would use *me* in extraordinary ways!

I mean no disrespect when I tongue-in-cheek intonate that I have often felt tricked or dragged into encounters that ultimately enriched my life. So by personal testimony, I can honestly say that if you invite Jehovah Sneaky to enlist you in his special forces, you will not be disappointed!

If you find yourself thinking, *"That's great for Marty or someone else, but not for me—I'm just ordinary."* I want to assure you that Jesus is in the business of taking ordinary people on extraordinary adventures. Just as Edmund, Lucy and Eustace in C.S. Lewis' *Voyage of the Dawn Treader* were pulled into an epic story through a vivid painting of a ship at sea, God wants to draw you into a life of purpose through the canvas of his Mission Accomplished!

Jesus, I do not want to give way to fear or cultivate a seed of unbelief. I want to follow you in faith—even if that means I'll have to confront the powers of darkness. I recognize that your power and your Spirit are within me. I recognize that greater are you in me, Jesus, than the enemy prowling about in the world. I'm praying now, asking you to sign me up for your agenda. Draw me into the story that you are writing for me. Amen.

Accomplish It!

- What does it mean to you, practically, to be the temple of the Holy Spirit?

- Have you walked in the awareness that you are engaged in a spiritual battle? Why or why not? How might this awareness affect your desire to advance God's kingdom?

- As you have read this book, have you sensed God's Spirit pulling you into a story that is bigger than yourself? In what ways?

- What do you think your next steps of obedience in this journey of faith might entail?

- What does it mean to become the answer to your own prayer?

Chapter 17

Holy Spirit Directed

With fear and trembling we must rely upon God
for guidance in the inner depths.
This is the sole way to walk according to the spirit.
— Watchman Nee

While speaking for a large youth conference in Bangalore, India, I welcomed an afternoon break and flagged down an auto rickshaw. Putt-putting down M.G. Road, I struck out on a mission to replace my wrist-watch battery that had just died. Arriving at the bustling marketplace, I jumped out, paid the driver and continued on foot into the mass of shoppers and merchants. Having previously noted a watch shop several blocks down, I maneuvered in that direction.

Still focused on my afternoon mission, I started to cross a narrow lane, lined with shops on either side, when Holy Spirit clearly nudged me to follow the lane rather than cross past it. Although a departure from my initial course, I didn't argue and turned right. Now, wandering an unfamiliar street I thought, *What next?* A half-beat later, the Lord replied, "Stop." I faced an Indian antiquities store (mind you, not one I would naturally choose to browse in), of which Holy Spirit directed, "Go in." I entered somewhat reluctantly, my eyes met by diverse tap-estries, wood carvings, hammered brass items and even a hefty carved, marble elephant—items obviously collected from various corners of this country and placed for sale. Moments later a slender and distinguished Indian woman addressed me in flawless English, "Hello, my name is Sarah; how might I be of assistance to you?"

I instantly surmised my Holy Spirit-directed mission. "'Sarah.' That's a beautiful name—similar to my daughter's name. I'm sure you must know that your name means 'princess'?" I began as a way of open-ing conversation.

"Please, come and sit by my desk. We must have chai," came her immediate response, and then, speaking something to a boy standing attentive nearby, she motioned for me to take my seat. Moments later the boy reappeared with a silver platter bearing a steaming silver kettle, two cups, a small dish of sugar cubes, and an assortment of biscuits, which he placed on Sarah's desk and hastily departed. Sarah poured the chai as we began our dialogue, which moved from the meaning of names to the origin of identity, namely that we are royal children of the King, created in his image. To reinforce the point, I handed Sarah my business card which simply read, "Marty Meyer" above my illustrious title, "Child of God," accompanied only by "1 John 3:1-3." Realizing that the Bible reference would be unfamiliar to her, I continued, "This refers to a Bible verse that says, 'How great is the love the Father has lavished on us, that we should be called children of God! And that is what we are!'" quoting the verse from memory.

Fascinated, Sarah launched into a stream of questions, prompting me to present her with a small evangelistic booklet[50] that I had created utilizing the fine artwork of my friend, Thomas Blackshear. She gazed at each depiction as I used the booklet to explain the Gospel. When my presentation concluded, I clarified the choice between life and death we all are responsible to make. "Sarah, what choice would you like to make?" I inquired.

She looked up from the leaflet, directly into my eyes, and with utmost sincerity pronounced, "Sir, I would like to make a choice for *life*." From that response we began to pray together. Sarah opened her heart and invited Jesus to be her Lord and Savior. That afternoon she discovered her true identity as a royal princess, daughter of the King of heaven.

My break time had expired but I had accomplished the real mission Jesus had scheduled for me at the market on M.G. Road. I left my Gospel booklet and business card with Sarah and returned to the youth conference. The following spring I received an envelope posted from India. It contained an Easter card and an elegant handwritten inscription thanking me for sharing the Good News. "Sir, for the first time I celebrated Easter and the new life I have in the resurrected Christ."

A year later I returned to the same city to conduct evangelism training for a mass of teens. One afternoon I made my way down M.G. Road to a certain store of Indian antiquities. Greeted by a fine-looking young shopkeeper, I inquired whether Sarah was available. "Oh, Sarah is gone traveling right now, acquiring other pieces for our shop." Then the junior manager leveled a question at me, "Are you the man with the Gospel booklet?" Taken aback by his direct query, I hesitated for just a moment. He clarified by opening Sarah's desk drawer, producing a leaflet, "Are you the man with *this* pamphlet?" Amazed, I nodded in affirmation and he continued. "Oh sir, it a pleasure to meet you. Sarah has told all of us about you. More importantly, she has shared this Good News message with us. Now, all of us that are Sarah's employees are followers of Jesus!"

Amazing events can unfold when we make an unexpected "right turn" in obedience to Holy Spirit's direction.

Step-by-Step Instructions

When reading the book of Acts, one gets a sense that Christ-followers were getting step-by-step instructions from Jesus. We should expect nothing less.

I picture Philip engaged in his routine of personal devotions when he began to receive step-by-step instructions for the day's assignment. The account is recorded in Acts 8:26-40: "Now an angel of the Lord said to Philip, 'Go south to the road—the desert road—that goes down from Jerusalem to Gaza.'" Philip received precise directions. At times we also may receive specific steps to follow, while at other times just a nudge or prompting. Regardless, it is of importance that we recognize when Holy Spirit is directing us and respond with obedience, as did Philip. "So he started out, and on his way he met an Ethiopian eunuch…" We need to simply *start out* and see what then unfolds. Philip met his divine appointment for the day, and so will we when we seek, recognize, and follow the Spirit's guidance.

After Philip took the first step, God then revealed the grander purpose and continued with giving instruction. "The Spirit told Philip, 'Go to that chariot and stay near it.'" Philip took that *next* step and an amazing story unfolded, resulting in a prominent Ethiopian coming to faith in Jesus Christ and receiving baptism in his name! We may never know the full impact of our simple acts of obedience in response to Holy Spirit's direction. Did you know that many in Ethiopia today trace their spiritual lineage back to this recorded Holy Spirit-directed encounter? Jesus has likewise prepared significant encounters for you and me, and is inviting us to listen and step out in obedience.

The story of Ananias, a formerly unknown disciple of Jesus, found its place into Scripture because he was a man who obeyed—albeit reluctantly—the Holy Spirit's direction. Acts 9:10-18 gives the full account, providing encouragement to unknown followers of Jesus, like us, to follow as God directs.

> In Damascus there was a disciple named Ananias. The Lord
> called to him in a vision, "Ananias!"

> "Yes, Lord," he answered.

> The Lord told him, "Go to the house of Judas on Straight Street
> and ask for a man from Tarsus named Saul, for he is praying. In
> a vision he has seen a man named Ananias come and place his
> hands on him to restore his sight."

It's noteworthy to point out here that God had orchestrated prior events to arrange for this divine appointment. Saul of Tarsus had planned to come to Damascus, the home city of Ananias, to search for believers to imprison, or worse! Jesus blinded Saul on the way there such that he had to be led like a child into the city, where he waited in darkness at Judas' home on Straight Street. Ananias' reluctance was admittedly understandable.

> "Lord," Ananias answered, "I have heard many reports about
> this man and all the harm he has done to your saints in
> Jerusalem. And he has come here with authority from the chief
> priests to arrest all who call on your name."

Have you ever tried to argue with God, even in the light of a clear directive? I certainly have, yet I'm grateful for every time I haven't argued and instead replied, "Yes."

> But the Lord said to Ananias, "Go! This man is my chosen in-
> strument to carry my name before the Gentiles and their kings
> and before the people of Israel. I will show him how much he
> must suffer for my name."

Ananias set his fear aside, saying "yes" to Jesus and the rest is history. The result of his Spirit-directed obedience? The salvation of the all-time greatest evangelist—redeeming his life and changing his name! You may not recall the name of Ananias, but I would bet that you've heard of the apostle Paul, author of nearly half the New Testament. You may never know this side of heaven, the outcome of your Spirit-directed steps of obedience. The Bible is replete with examples to teach us that the Shepherd offers step-by-step instruction through his Spirit, placed within us. We should expect nothing less.

Holy Spirit Will Prepare the Way

Our YWAM ministry in Idaho had recently launched a Backpackers' Discipleship Training School.[51] Zach, the fiery bearded leader in his mid-twenties and his small team of rugged trekkers had just returned home from their first outreach to nomadic herdsmen of northern Mongolia.

I couldn't wait to hear of the adventures and scheduled time to meet with Zach just days after his return. I poured hot tea for him and black coffee for myself and we settled onto the back deck of the Depot, an old restored train station now used as our YWAM missionary training and sending center. We enjoyed the warmth of direct sunlight through chilly air, and the spectacular view of the Payette River with its backdrop of forested peaks. Zach began his story with typical wild-eyed enthusiasm.

Marty, it was incredible! We were in the mountainous highlands of northern Mongolia, and continually asking Father where he wanted us to go next. Our focus was reaching nomadic tribes with the Gospel, but it was late November, when they are moving from their summer locations to places where they winter. The Mongols live in *gers*, which are round tents constructed with collapsible wooden lattices for the structure, and poles supporting yak-hide coverings. When it's time to change seasonal locations, they fold up their houses, put them on carts and move. But it made it difficult for us to find them during this time.

Steve, Andy, Lucas and I had loaded into our rented four-wheel drive van along with our driver, our translator, and 500 Mongolian Bibles. We were intent on searching for nomadic Mongolian families so that we could share the Gospel and present Bibles, but first we had to find them! We had been driving every day for one week across the high plateau tundra and wanted to make it over the mountain range by nightfall. But by early afternoon we encountered a snowstorm impeding our progress. By late afternoon the storm had developed into a full-on blizzard and any hope of following the faint route was lost under a fresh blanketing of snow.

We didn't know what to do. The temperature had dropped to below zero and we wondered if we should just turn back. We decided to pray and ask Jesus where to go and what to do next. We silenced our own voices—and that of the enemy—and asked the Holy Spirit to guide us. After a time of waiting I asked my companions if they had received any direction. Nothing. So, we went back to prayer and I saw in my mind's eye a three-dimensional arrow pointing north. When I shared this picture with the others, we collectively accepted this as clear guidance, so I instructed the driver to turn 45 degrees to the right and follow the bobbling compass on the dashboard, due north.

After a nervous hour of driving with only thirty feet of visibility, it started to get dark. Naturally we all began to question whether I was certain that what I had received was really from the Lord. But deep down I felt confident it was, so we stayed the course and continued north. Another 45 minutes of driving blind passed, when we stopped the van and prayed, "Lord, are you sure you want us to keep going, or should we stop and turn around?" We clearly sensed that we were to continue onward, so the van lurched forward again. Within only two minutes from that point, our headlights lit upon a brightly-painted door of a *ger*. Had our driver not hit the brakes, our van would have plowed into their living room! An older Mongolian man emerged, approached our vehicle looking puzzled, and then motioned us to come inside for shelter.

It was midnight when our team piled into the cozy circular room and we immediately began to thaw by the warmth of the small dung-burning stove. Lighted candles added to the warm glow and the man's wife soon provided yak-butter tea served in simple tin vessels. We made introductions with the help of our interpreter, but while our obvious question was, *What on earth are we doing way out here?* their question I suppose was, *Why are four Americans sitting in our ger?*

I explained that we had prayed to our God and he had specifically led us directly to their home. Upon hearing this, the woman began to speak with the translator at length in a flurry of excited tones. We simply waited. When she was finished, the translator, himself a believer, spoke with equally enthused intonation. "This woman explained that last night she had a dream. In the dream four foreign men arrived at her home and they had a very important book. From her dream she was shown that this book of truth would transform her life and the life of her entire family. She is asking if you have brought them a book?"

My team members could hardly believe what we were hearing! This was extraordinary! But then again, isn't that exactly like our God—to prepare the way before us? Immediately I braved the blizzard to retrieve a Mongolian Bible from the van. Presenting it to the husband and his wife we said that this was the entire reason we had come, to bring the Truth contained in this book.

We took turns sharing the biblical narrative, beginning with Creation and pausing to let them ask questions. The man kept the dialogue going as his wife continued to toss chips of dung into the stove. This conversation continued into the earliest morning hours until we succumbed to the kind invitation to sleep and bedded down for the brief remainder of that night.

When we awoke, the man was waiting patiently, and greeted us with more yak-butter tea. He told us that he had stayed up pondering the things we had shared with them. Through our translator he asked, "I only have one remaining question. How is it that when Jesus died on the cross and rose from the dead…how is it that this brings salvation to me now?" The man and woman listened intently as we addressed this and all their remaining questions to what seemed their satisfaction. Then, matter-of-factly, the father made this announcement:

"I believe you. I believe everything you have told us. You were sent by God to bring us the truth and to give us his book. We want to follow Jesus. Can you pray for us now?"

A glorious time of prayer followed as this precious couple in the far-reaches of Mongolia invited Jesus to be their Savior, committing to know him and follow him through his book of truth.

When our prayer concluded, the wife immediately responded with a question.

"What about this?" she inquired, pointing to her makeshift Buddhist shrine atop a crude wooden crate. The box was draped with linen and ornamented with a squatty framed picture of the Buddha, short burning candles, and small dishes of food presented as an offering. "Now that I have Jesus, do I still need this?"

We reiterated that Jesus is the only God, and following him is exclusive. No one beside the One who gave his life for us is worthy of our praise and adoration. That explanation seemed good enough for the woman and she promptly gathered up all the items on her mobile shrine, opened the painted door of the *ger* and chucked them out into the fresh depths of snow. The father nodded his approval, saying, "We will tell all of our children about the truth we have received. I have made a decision for my entire clan, from this day forward our family will all follow Jesus."

By this time on the back deck my coffee was cold and untouched, my having been enrapt in Zach's narrative. We sat for moments longer, soaking in the beauty of our Idaho range and praising God for those he rescued in the mountains of Mongolia. What wonders occur when we follow Holy Spirit's direction!

Where God Guides, He Provides!

A popular saying among missionaries is, "Where God guides, he provides," perhaps because many of us are woefully underfunded, yet not inclined to limit God based on lacking resources. If God is truly calling us to go somewhere or do something, we regard it as his responsibility to get us there and do it through us.

My friend, Ross Tooley, shares a story in his book, *Adventures in Naked Faith*,[52] about traveling around the world with only the coins in his pocket. My colleague, Kel Steiner, tells similar tales in *Adventures in Saying Yes to God*,[53] of Jesus providing access and even assistance from military troops, to reach a tribe with the Gospel on a remote island in the South Pacific. I've recounted some of my own stories of God's miraculous provision in my book *Epic Faith*.[54] What do we all have in common? We had to seek and then take a step of *faith*, partnering it with *obedience*, when trusting that God would provide for the journey just as he promised.

> [Jesus] told them: "Take nothing for the journey—no staff, no bag, no bread, no money, no extra tunic. Whatever house you enter, stay there until you leave that town." (Luke 9:3-4)

In reading this book you may be inspired to do something way beyond your means. It is time to join the litany of faithful saints who have preceded you and take a leap into the faithful arms of Jesus, trusting that he will also provide for *you*!

One thing proves certain, when you follow the direction of the Holy Spirit and trust Jesus to provide for your journey, you will find yourself in the right place at the right time for the right reason to be a purposeful vessel in the hands of the Master.

The Right Place at the Right Time

Back in my younger years as a youth pastor, Kelly and I were leading our youth group on a mission trip to Mexicali, Mexico. One morning our day's "planned" ministry in Mexicali fell through. Though ready to share the Gospel, our team didn't know where to go or what to do. I had an impression that rather than a disappointment; this could be an exciting adventure in expectation—to trust that God had planned something different...perhaps better. We simply had to ask him for his agenda, and then follow it.

I instructed the students that we would pray and ask God where we should go and what to do, though frankly uncertain how this exercise might work since "hearing God's voice" was not something taught or practiced in our conservative tradition. During the prayer I personally drew a blank, but feigned confidence by asking the youth, "Okay, what did you hear from the Lord?"

Tiffany started by saying, "I heard, 'Go south.'"

"I also got the word 'south,'" shouted Jason.

"Me too," exclaimed another.

Kelly and I looked at each other a bit sheepishly, "Okay, south it is." In a moment we were packed into our fifteen-passenger van, pointed south. We soon found ourselves out of the crowded city center and bumping along on a washboard road in the middle of a desert. I'm not going to lie: I was thinking, *We've made a terrible mistake. There's no one out here to witness to. Parents are going to kill me!*

After rambling for over an hour through arid desolation, I pulled the van over and opened my well-worn atlas. We were not "lost" *per se*, because I could tell *where* we were; it's just that nothing else was anywhere out there. Not a town or colonia for miles. "Okay gang, I'm wondering if maybe we should pray again." We all bowed our heads in silence. Then I tentatively prompted the students to share any impressions they felt they had received.

"Okay....?"

"Yep, we're on the right track," one youth offered.

"Keep going south," another piped in. "Just keep driving, Marty. Just keep on driving!"

So I did, navigating south across the desert for another three hours! We finally encountered the Gulf of California and discovered the coastal community of San Felipe. *Now we're talking!* A truly authentic Mexican town before us, we assumed that this was exactly where God had directed our team. Immediately we pulled over near a busy intersection, set up our sound system, and launched into a drama followed by testimonies and preaching. We had barely concluded our open-air evangelism event when a Mexican pastor pulled up in a van. He jumped out and beelined toward me.

"What are you guys doing *here?* he questioned. "Don't you know that everyone is waiting for you at the church? We were supposed to start an hour ago, and our worship leader is starting to run out of songs. Come on, follow me to the church."

I intended to protest, trying to cut in about the apparent miscommunication—that we were not the team he was expecting. But he wouldn't listen. "We can talk about all that later. Please, just get in your van and follow me to the church," the pastor insisted.

"Okay, everybody," I shouted to our team, "Let's get packed up and loaded in the van quickly. It looks like God has just given us our next assignment!"

In no time we were racing to keep up with the pastor's van, hurrying and scurrying through winding city streets. We arrived at a large church, completely packed with an audience obviously weary of singing.

"Okay, it's your turn," the pastor prompted, hurriedly motioning us to the front. My team, now familiar with the routine, set up and launched into their well-executed drama-testimony-puppet-preaching Gospel presentation, complete with altar call.

While this was going on, the pastor received a phone call and took it in the room behind us. Kelly and I soon realized that the call came from an apologetic ministry coordinator, informing him that his expected team would *not* be coming. We could overhear the one-sided conversation.

"No, they are *here!*" the pastor demanded. "Thank you for sending the team. They are fantastic. The people especially love the puppet show and the dramas! Thank you so much for sending such a great evangelism team for our big annual revival meeting!"

"On second thought, maybe we shouldn't tell him," Kelly whispered to me with a wink and a smile.

When listening to the Holy Spirit and following his direction you might just find yourself in exactly the right place at the right time. You'll enjoy the delight of it, while Jesus gets all the glory for making it happen.

Jesus, I'm excited for the next adventure you have prepared for me. I confess that my own voice of reason can make it difficult to listen to your still, small voice. I desire to get tuned in to the Holy Spirit. I will be waiting and listening, and trust that in the next few days you are going to prompt me with directions to my own divine appointment. When you do, give me the courage to obey. Amen.

Accomplish It!

- What do Bible stories like the ones shared here of Philip and Ananias teach us about being open to the direction of the Holy Spirit?

- What could you do to cultivate a supple attitude towards the Holy Spirit's guidance?

- Order copies of the tract, "Are You Forgiven," that Marty used to share the Gospel with Sarah (https://epicfaith.net). Keep extra Bibles and resources like this on hand in expectation of Holy Spirit-directed appointments.

- How might the understanding that the Holy Spirit goes before us, preparing the way, help us walk in faith and confidence?

- Invite Jesus to bring a divine appointment into your life this week!

Chapter 18

No Matter the Cost

For whoever wants to save his life will lose it, but whoever loses his life for me and for the Gospel will save it.
— Jesus Christ

Revenge or Forgiveness?

I returned several years later to the hills of Asaam, India with a team of students to work with Pastor Puna (from chapter 11) and the Amri Karbi people group. Pastor assigned one of his young Karbi disciples, Jayanta, to serve my team as translator and guide. At 19 years of age, Jayanta wasn't much older than the students he was positioned to lead. His strong frame was matched by a broad infectious smile that quickly established a fond place in each of our hearts. Our team moved from village to village sharing the Gospel and encouraging believers, Jayanta always in the thick of it while interpreting for our team. One afternoon rain fell so hard that the roofline of the church created a wide natural "shower." Jayanta grabbed a bottle of shampoo and our entire team took outside showers fully clothed, replete in hilarity!

One free afternoon I found myself with Jayanta sitting under a banana tree. We had harvested some of the fruit, and were stripping peels and devouring them. I posed a serious question for my cheerful young friend. "Jayanta, I will understand if you don't want to talk about it...," I cautioned, "but Pastor Puna shared with me that your older brother was one of the new believers martyred for his faith. How did you and your family handle that, and how have you captured such a joyful disposition?"

He paused in sober contemplation for a while before he began, "Marty, I should probably first explain how it happened. My whole family came to Jesus through Pastor Puna's ministry. We had been following Jesus for only three years when some of the young men in our village started really giving us trouble. At first these guys would question,

'Why are you following this foreign god? Return to the ways of your people!' But then they began to taunt and even threaten us, 'If you don't turn away from this Jesus we will give you a beating you'll never forget.' One day as my older brother and I were walking back from the market-place we were stopped by this gang on the road and they would not let us pass. They threatened my brother, 'Curse Jesus or we will kill you.' You could see the hate in their eyes, but my brother, Provin, would not compromise. He was a strong and lean twenty-one-year-old at this time but was no match for a mob of such angry young men. When Provin said he would never deny his Savior Jesus, the men became violent. The confrontation started with shoving, but when Provin fell down, they picked up stones and sticks and began to beat him without mercy."

I felt the pain with Jayanta as he somberly shared this tragic story. There was a depth to this young man that obviously sourced his infectious joy. He continued,

"Marty, I felt so helpless; I was only fourteen years old. I was afraid and I ran all the way home to call for my father. By the time we returned we found Provin's lifeless, bloody body on the road.

"When I saw him, my tears ran hot with rage. The faces of my brothers' killers were seared into my memory and I determined that very day that I would make revenge upon them someday. I knew that this is not what Jesus would want me to do, but I didn't care; I was fueled by one thing—those murderers would die for what they did to my brother. I began making trips into the city to take classes in martial arts and I lifted weights constantly, all the while thinking that as soon as I was big enough and strong enough, those men would pay for what they had done. One morning I went out into the forest just to be alone. I was sitting on a very large rock when suddenly I was confronted by the voice of Jesus: 'Jayanta, are you going to follow me or are you going to follow your anger and revenge? You cannot follow both. Which path will you choose?'

"It had been so long since I had prayed. For the previous four years I was consumed with vengeance. How could I just let that go? How could I forgive those who were so undeserving? Then I saw a picture in my mind of Jesus on his cross for someone so undeserving...like me. I knew I must decide, or I would become lost in my anger—I would become like those I hated. 'Jesus, I choose to follow you with all my heart. I'm giving you my pain and rage. Take away my hatred of these men.' As soon as I prayed those words I felt a literal weight being lifted off my shoulders. I was even able to finally genuinely grieve for my brother. Since then I have discovered that my true joy is found by submitting to and serving Jesus, the One my brother also loved so dearly."

Surprised by Suffering

How are we, as believers, to carry out the Great Commission in the face of suffering and persecution? When Jayanta shifted his focus from his suffering to the cross of Jesus, he found full freedom from his anger and lust for revenge. At some point, each of us must come to understand that persecution was forewarned to us, even stated as something to be expected.

Dear friends, do not be surprised at the painful trial you are suffering, as though something strange were happening to you. But rejoice that you participate in the sufferings of Christ, so that you may be overjoyed when his glory is revealed. If you are insulted because of the name of Christ, you are blessed, for the Spirit of glory and of God rests on you. (1 Pet. 4:12-14)

Like I've previously said, many in the West have adopted the mistaken theology that God's primary concern is for our comfort, happiness and prosperity. This errant perspective leaves us surprised by suffering and perplexed at persecution. Yet Jesus himself promised trouble in the work of Christ and for the sake of the Gospel!

Blessed are you when people insult you, persecute you and falsely say all kinds of evil against you because of me. Rejoice and be glad, because great is your reward in heaven, for in the same way they persecuted the prophets who were before you. (Matt. 5:11-12)

I have told you these things, so that in me you may have peace. In this world you will have trouble. But take heart! I have overcome the world. (John 16:33)

In his book *The Insanity of Obedience*, Nik Ripkin, from his vast research of Christians in persecution, reminds us that for the majority of believers around the world, suffering for the name of Jesus is *normal*! In fact, persecution inevitably arises as a natural byproduct when individuals receive and respond to the Gospel.

If our goal were simply to reduce persecution, that could easily be done. The way to reduce persecution—or the way to eliminate persecution completely—is simply to keep people from coming into relationship with Jesus. If our goal were simply to stop persecution, then followers of Jesus could accomplish that goal easily and quickly by refusing to share Jesus—by refusing to live as sheep among wolves.

Obviously, that is something that we are not willing to do! Hopefully, believers are not willing to stop sharing their faith. Even so, this is a good reminder that the primary cause of persecution is people coming into relationship with Jesus. Perhaps it is good to be reminded that, given our calling and our mission, the reduction (or elimination) of persecution is not our ultimate goal.[55]

Is it Safe?

Many of us approach the Great Commission with the prerequisite question, "Is it safe?" In our insular Western culture we have prioritized safety above obedience. Once my friend Dan and I were planning to visit a region that strictly forbade open preaching of the Gospel. Yet that was precisely our undeterred intent.

The day before leaving for this trip, I walked up to the prayer chapel to spend some time with Jesus. Within moments I found myself in the Lord's presence accompanied by a strong assurance that God desired my participation on this trip. Then immediately, like watching a movie in my mind's eye, I saw myself on a stage preaching the Gospel to the masses in this restricted area. I finished preaching and stepped down to begin praying for individuals but was met by a group of stern police officers. I envisioned them putting handcuffs on me, shoving me into a car, and driving me off to jail. In my vision they forcefully threw me into a dank cell, and when I heard the iron door snap shut, I sensed the Shepherd's voice clearly ask, "Marty, would you choose this?"

The question did not seem close to hypothetical in that moment. In all honesty, within the comfortable confines of those hallowed prayer chapel walls I struggled through my own fear, and then with apprehension at how foreign imprisonment would affect Kelly—and our toddler son and newborn daughter. The anxiety of it caused me to question, *Maybe Jesus is warning me to cancel the trip.*

It is revealing how influenced I had been by a worldly, Western-Christian mindset—to interpret the possibility of imprisonment as a warning to retreat. My initial response shone a light on my false belief system: *Certainly Jesus wouldn't want* **me** *to* **suffer** *for the Gospel.*

But why not?

As I wrestled with fear, my focus began shifting to the suffering of my Savior. I thought of Jesus' ultimate sacrifice on the cross to free me from sin and reconcile me to the Father. Though indescribably difficult, I could give no other response:

"Yes, Lord. I will choose this. If you want me to preach the Gospel, the answer is 'yes.' If that means being jailed for you, the answer is 'yes.' How could I withhold anything from you when you have given everything for me? Yes, Lord, I choose you."

The issue was settled in my own heart, but I knew I had to I return home to pray with my wife. Kelly listened, understandably agitated as I described everything I had just envisioned and fought through in the chapel. She held tightly to my hand and managed, "I'm proud of you." Then with dripping eyes and no other words to manage, she began to pray, "Jesus, I release my husband to you and into your care. I ask that you bring him home safely to me and our children, but if you have another purpose for his life, I release him to be obedient to you."[56]

I went on that God-ordained trip with confidence and preached the Gospel as planned. Almost surprisingly, I returned home without incident. Circumstances had not been entirely safe, yet from the day the issue was settled in our hearts, I proceeded willingly and obediently to Jesus, regardless of outcome. I believe this is a vitally important matter that all of God's children must resolve.

The real question is not, "Is it safe?" but rather, "Is Jesus worthy?"

Sheep Among Wolves

Jesus once uttered a troubling phrase when sending out his followers on a Gospel-proclaiming mission; perhaps a phrase that we would prefer to skip over and ignore. Nevertheless, in these recorded words we can find a profound connection between our mission and his.

After this the Lord appointed seventy-two others and sent them two by two ahead of him to every town and place where he was about to go. He told them, "The harvest is plentiful, but the workers are few. Ask the Lord of the harvest, therefore, to send out workers into his harvest field. *Go! I am sending you out like lambs among wolves.*" (Luke 10:1-3)

Jesus sending out his faithful followers like lambs among wolves? I don't know about you, but I don't like that. *I don't want to be the lamb! Are you serious, Jesus? I live in mountain ranchlands…I know what wolves do to lambs!* Even so, this mirrors exactly how Jesus came to us. Upon seeing Jesus, John the Baptist prophetically proclaimed, "Look, the *Lamb* of God, who takes away the sin of the world!" (John 1:29)

Jesus does not flippantly send us out to the wolves. He goes with us. Jesus set the example as the Lamb of God, giving his life as the ultimate sacrifice for sin. By his resurrection he proved that death is no victor and he promised that neither could it defeat us. After his glorious resurrection, Jesus proclaimed "Peace be with you! As the Father has sent me, I am sending you." (John 20:21) His followers were terrified, so Jesus gave them peace. His peace enables us to proceed confidently as lambs, even among wolves. Jesus sends us out in the same manner that he was sent by his Father.

Prior to going to the cross, Jesus spoke plainly about his lamb-like mission. "He then began to teach them that the Son of Man must suffer many things and be rejected by the elders, chief priests and teachers of the law, and that he must be killed and after three days rise again. He spoke plainly about this, and Peter took him aside and began to rebuke him." (Mark 8:31-32)

How often do we play the part of Peter, asserting, "Suffering is not part of God's agenda?" Yet clearly it is—for Jesus *and* for us. Jesus confronts Peter (and us) on worldly thinking. "You do not have in mind the things of God, but the things of men." (Mark 8:33) Jesus continued by addressing all who would follow him:

> Then he called the crowd to him along with his disciples and said: "If anyone would come after me, he must *deny himself* and *take up his cross* and *follow me.* For whoever wants to save his life will lose it, but whoever loses his life for me and for the Gospel will save it. What good is it for a man to gain the whole world, yet *forfeit his soul*?" (Mark 8:34-36)

To argue that suffering is not necessary in God's plan is dishonest, and to the degree that we forget who we are, denying that we are appointed to share in the suffering of Christ. Jesus clearly calls us to follow in his footsteps, which undeniably includes sacrifice. Jesus is not only our friend and good Shepherd, but also the fiery King of heaven who deserves our worship, allegiance and surrender.

Jesus is Worthy

My friend, Bharat, is a missionary in a major city in north India. He has taken on the project of training pastors who were formerly operating under a traditional paradigm, to instead adopt a reproducible church-planting model. Many pastors who have simply been "tending the flock" are now *equipping* their flock to go mingle with the wolves. Philip was one of these Indian pastors who found his greater potential through Bharat's training and began weekly trips to a Jat village, attempting to plant a house church there. The Jat remains one of the thirty-one largest Frontier People Groups in desperate need of the Gospel.[57] I had been following Pastor Philip's efforts via Bharat's prayer updates and was devastated to learn that Philip had been attacked in the Jat village for preaching the Gospel. Beaten with rods and stones, taking many severe blows to the head, he was literally left for dead. Philip regained consciousness, bleeding and lying in a ditch, but managed to recover his flip phone from his pocket and call his wife. She was able to retrieve him and rush him to the hospital, where he spent several days in intensive care. Receiving the email report from Bharat, I began to pray for Philip's extensive recovery.

This past January I visited Bharat in India and he invited me to speak for his pastors' leadership training seminar. I felt humbled by the privilege to teach these servants of Jesus when in truth I had much to learn from them. After the formal instruction time, Bharat invited me to pray for each one who desired to receive a blessing. Several leaders came forward with specific prayer requests and I anointed them with oil, imparting an empowerment of the Holy Spirit upon their lives. The last pastor came forward with his wife. I noticed that he was limping, and further marked by a large dent in his skull, partially closing his left eye. "Brother, please pray for my wife and me that we will have boldness and courage as we proclaim the Good News of Jesus in a nearby Jat village. Some time ago I was brutally beaten for sharing my faith, but as soon as I was released from the hospital I returned to the same village to continue preaching of the love and forgiveness available in our Lord

Jesus Christ. Brother, remember us in your prayers: my name is Philip."
Praise be to God.

For Philip, Jesus is worthy of his willingness to go as a lamb among
wolves.

As I have said previously, we find our greatest fulfillment by aligning
our lives with Jesus' final mandate. We discover who God has created us
to be through pursuit of his purpose. Our identity is acutely revealed in
the face of adversity, suffering and persecution. Through these we verify
the genuineness of our faith. A litany of martyrs has gone before us,
proclaiming that Jesus is worthy, even at the cost of their own lives.
Polycarp, the beloved bishop of Smyrna (present day Turkey), was once
afforded the opportunity to go free if only he would curse Christ. His
famous response is recorded in *Foxe's Book of Martyrs*, "Eighty and six
years have I served him, and he never once wronged me; how then shall
I blaspheme my King, who hath saved me?" For this he was burned at
the stake and run through with the sword.[58]

We must ask ourselves the difficult questions, *Would I curse Christ
under such circumstances? Would I choose my freedom by denying the Lord?*
Of course not, we insist. Yet whenever we have muffled our voices in fear
of the world, haven't we already denied him and submitted ourselves to
fear's bondage?

Author and pastor, John Piper, challenges us to take bold risk, even
in the face of suffering, to see the love of Jesus extended to those who
hate him.

> When the threat of death becomes a door to paradise the final
> barrier to temporal risk is broken. When a Christian says from
> the heart, "To live is Christ and to die is gain," he is free to love
> no matter what. Some forms of radical Islam may entice mar-
> tyr-murderers with similar dreams, but Christian hope is the
> power to love, not kill. Christian hope produces life-givers, not
> life-takers. The crucified Christ calls his people to live and die
> for their enemies, as he did. The only risks permitted by Christ
> are the perils of love. ". . .love your enemies, do good to those
> who hate you, bless those who curse you, pray for those who
> abuse you."[59] (Luke 6:27-28)

Jesus will forever be praised as the Lamb of God and we will someday join in the heavenly chorus exclaiming, ". . .Worthy is the Lamb,

who was slain, to receive power and wealth and wisdom and strength and honor and glory and praise!" (Rev. 5:12). Jesus is calling us to live triumphant lives, proclaiming Christ even as lambs among the wolves.

Forgiveness is Victorious Over Fear

Our time among the Amri Karbi people was drawing to a close and my entire team would miss these people who had become precious to us. For our final day of outreach, Jayenta had reserved a local school auditorium for a grand outreach program. We spent the entire day in preparations, canvasing the surrounding area and inviting all to our special event. We prepared a drama set to music, powerfully presenting the Gospel. Students had been rehearsing their testimonies of Jesus' transformational work in their own lives, and I had been fine-tuning a message to concisely share the work of Jesus on our behalf, along with a pointed invitation to respond to his Good News offer. As the evening approached people began streaming in from surrounding villages, completely packing out the auditorium.

In my final moments of prayer prior to taking the stage, Jayanta returned from surveying the crammed venue, visibly shaken. With trembling voice and pale expression he announced, "I cannot translate for you and your team tonight, Marty. I'm sorry, I just cannot do it." Jayanta did not explain any further but I assumed his nerves were the culprit on account of such a large crowd. "Jayanta, you *must* translate for us! You are the only one who can do it. You have translated for us every day for the past two weeks and have done such an excellent job. You will be fine. Let me pray for you right now, that Jesus will give you the courage to do it."

After saying, "Amen," Jayanta really had no choice but to reluctantly follow me out onto the stage and translate as planned. Nevertheless, it seemed that a burden weighed heavily upon him throughout the program.

The evening progressed fantastically. Children and adults smiled broadly as they took in our theatrical presentations. The audience connected with our teens who gave heartfelt testimonies alongside Jayanta as he carefully interpreted, communicating not only words, but with the passion in which they were spoken. Finally, to close, I stepped beside my young friend and spoke of the Father's love and forgiveness available through Jesus Christ. Side-by-side we implored a rapt audience to be reconciled to God. "Forgiveness is available regardless of your past. When you turn to Jesus you are made new and come into the unconditionally loving arms of the Father." Harmoniously Jayanta and I delivered these words, which brought tears to both of our eyes.

During the program I had noticed a group of rough-looking, agitated men standing against the farthest back wall. They had appeared intent on causing trouble when they arrived, but as the Gospel came forth repeatedly throughout the night, they seemed to soften. In particular, our final message on forgiveness seemed to touch them deeply. When the crowd was given the invitation to respond to the Gospel, these ruffians began a walk of contrition straight to the front of the stage, some even weeping as they came. The front of the auditorium became packed with people desiring to receive forgiveness and a new relationship with the Father. Our youth team encompassed the penitent as Jayanta led in prayer, inviting Jesus to become Lord and Savior of broken lives and subsequent dedications to following the one true God.

It was impossible to not feel the tangible smile of the Father and the rejoicing of angels in the events of that night, ushering children of God back into reconciliation with their Father. Jayanta was deeply moved also, but in a manner and for reasons I could not readily discern. We found a place to talk later, my eyes asking the question that Jayanta's heart was bursting to share. "Marty, I didn't think I could do it. I didn't know if I could *truly* forgive and honestly share God's message of forgiveness tonight. I did not want to stand in front of that crowd and translate because I saw among the audience—standing in the back—the men who killed my brother..."

I was dumbfounded as Jayanta continued, "Even as we stood together sharing the Gospel on stage, I realized that the forgiveness that I had received from Jesus extended even to these guilty ones. It was Jesus who enabled me to look right into their eyes as we spoke words of forgiveness over them. Marty, those men who I had spent years hating and plotting revenge against, were the first to respond to Jesus' invitation to receive forgiveness tonight...they are now my brothers in Christ." At that point Jayanta folded into my arms and released a deep well of emotion that had been pent up far too long inside his heart. A deep work had transpired in my young brother's life. Forgiveness had conquered fear and hatred.

That evening, Jayanta discovered his identity in Christ in a profound way. By fully surrendering his own life to Jesus, he became the kind of person who could look his brother's killers straight in the eyes and grace them with love and forgiveness through his faith in Christ.

Father is also inviting you to discover the kind of person he has created you to be. When you say "yes" to God and align your purposes to his, rather than forfeiting your life, you instead discover your true self. When you push through your fears, you will experience widened dimensions of fulfillment as you live to see the Lord Jesus' mission accomplished.

Jesus is Calling You

Father is calling you to step into your destiny, but the giants of fear, unbelief, insecurity, and pride attempt to block the gate. We must break through in victory to possess the lands to which he has called us.

Strangely, one of God's greatest servants uttered some of the saddest words recorded in the Bible. God had presented a hefty and difficult job—similar to the task of completing the Great Commission. He prepared a particular person for this task, investing more than forty years in the training process. In his perfect timing, God revealed the task: the liberation of his children, the nation of Israel, from the captivity of cruel Egyptian oppressors. This could be viewed as quite similar to *our* calling of bringing freedom from darkness through the light of the Gospel to the unreached. God called this biblical person that he had prepared for the job: Moses—just as Jesus has called and empowered you and me to share his message that brings life and freedom.

Regrettably, when God called Moses, instead of getting obedience he heard excuses. "I'm not worthy. I'm not cut out for the job. What if nobody believes me?" Finally, when Moses ran out of excuses, he uttered these pathetic words: "O Lord, please send someone else to do it." (Exod. 4:10) It's not an easy question for me to ask, but have you ever uttered something similar in regard to the Great Commission? Emptied of excuses, have you resigned to the sad but honest truth—that you are unwilling? "Just send somebody else, God."

I'm thankful that God has not accepted my own initial reluctance as my final answer. He has given grace upon grace to me. My destiny *and* the lives of captives hang in the balance, awaiting my willing obedient response. God's reply to Moses is his same admonition to you and me, "I didn't call somebody else: I CALLED YOU!"

I implore you, brothers and sisters in Christ, do not miss out on the miraculous parting, in which God makes a way where there is none.

Don't miss the plentiful manna provided by God when you step out in faith beyond your capacity. Don't miss your promised inheritance because you fear the giants standing in the way. Embrace God's call on your life and walk in the divine purposes he has prepared for you!

You have come to the end of this book, but its stories are far from finished. *Your* steps of obedience will write new chapters. Together we will co-labor to see his mission accomplished, on earth as it is in heaven!

In the final section that follows, you will find Great Commission Partners fiercely committed to equipping you for your unique role in finishing the task. I beg of you, diligently turn through these next pages, asking Holy Spirit to highlight those with which you are to participate. Whether you are sensing God's leading to pray, tell, send, go, stay, or multiply, these Great Commission Partners are experienced and eager to provide believers with ample engagement opportunities.

Jesus, I commit to following you with my whole life, embracing the destiny you have for me. Hear am I, Lord, send me. I have a deep gratitude for your love and forgiveness and want to share it with the whole world. I want to align my life with your purposes. Holy Spirit, show me my next steps and with which Great Commission Partners you want me to engage. I trust that you will give me direction as I fix my focus onto you. You are worthy! Amen. All glory to the King and his Son!

Accomplish It!

- Surrender your life completely to Jesus—even if that means experiencing discomfort or persecution for the cause of Christ.

- Prayerfully read through the following "Great Commission Partners" section. Commit to contacting several of these organizations and inquiring how you might engage with them to complete the Great Commission.

- Continue your journey by reading *Epic Faith*, available at https:// epicfaith.net. Lead a small group utilizing the "Epic Faith Adventure Guide" and corresponding "Leader's Edition."

Contributor Acknowledgements

The concept for the pie charts in Figures 2 & 4 displayed on the first two pages of the Great Commission Partner section was originated by the late Dr. Ralph Winter. FrontierVentures.org (formerly the U.S. Center for World Mission) published the original chart and Dr. Winter's legacy is now carried on by his daughter R.W. Lewis. Data for the current charts were compiled by Chris Maynard of TransformingInformation. com using data from Joshua Project and Operation World. The information in Figures 2 & 4 appears in the article by R.W. Lewis, "Clarifying the Remaining Frontier Mission Task," *International Journal of Frontier Missiology* (35:4, Winter 2018), 158-159.

Endnotes

1. *Barna report*, "Translating the Great Commission," (March 27, 2018).

2. See Matthew 20:1-16.

3. Adapted from *Epic Faith* (YWAM Publishing: Seattle, 2016), 105-106.

4. John Bunyan, *Pilgrim's Progress* (London, 1678).

5. I highly recommend reading Joy Dawson's books. Her love and zeal for God is contagious.

6. Joy Dawson, *The Character of the One Who Says "Go"*, (YWAM Publishing: Seattle,1986), 6.

7. Adapted from *Epic Faith* (YWAM Publishing: Seattle, 2016), 55-60.

8. *Webster's New World Dictionary* (The World Publishing Company, 1964).

9. "Religion that God our Father accepts as pure and faultless is this: to look after orphans and widows in their distress and to keep oneself from being polluted by the world." (James 1:27)

10. See Appendix, Figures 3 & 4.

11. "The Joshua Project" https://joshuaproject.net (accessed September 2018).

12. Luke 2:25-35.

13. John Piper, *Let the Nations Be Glad! The Supremacy of God in Missions* (Grand Rapids: Baker, 1993/2003), 35.

14. Tom Zawaki, "Emancipation of the Freed: Exploring the Fullness of Freedom," http://emancipationofthefreed.blogspot.com/2007/01/john-leonard-dober-and-david-nitschman.html (20 January 2007, accessed September 2018).

15. See John 1:1-14. John's poetic gospel describes Jesus as the "word" who became flesh to dwell with the people he created. His mission gives us access to be reconciled children of God.

16. Adapted from *Epic Faith* (YWAM Publishing: Seattle, 2016), 104.

17. Originally published in *Epic Faith* (YWAM Publishing: Seattle, 2016), 106-108.

18. N|P Source, "The Ultimate List Of Online Giving Statistics For 2018," https://nonprofitssource.com/online-giving-statistics (accessed October 2018).

19. *Barna Report*, "Translating the Great Commission" (March 27, 2018).

20. Peter Greer, Chris Horst, *Mission Drift: The Unspoken Crisis Facing Leaders, Charities, and Churches* (Bethany House Publishers: Bloomington, MN, 2014), 71-72.

21. Bruce Wilkinson, *The Dream Giver*, (Multnomah Publishers: Danvers, MA, 2009).

22. Some suggested organizations and programs: http://www.missionadventures.net, http://multmove.net/go31/. https://pray15days.org. https://www.30daysprayer.com. https://www.harvestfrontiers.org, and https://www.ttionline.org.

23. In the years that have passed since our trek through the jungle, I have recalled Miguel's stories as a single narrative. When I asked Miguel and Marlien to verify this account they clarified that while the details are accurate, my recollection had combined elements from several different events.

24. Ron Boehme, *The Fourth Wave* (YWAM Publishing: Seattle, 2011), 94.

25. 24:14; https://www.2414now.net.

26. Bob Creson, "What's Been Accomplished and What Remains" *Mission Frontiers* (40:5, 2018), 6-11.

27. Loren Cunningham, *We Can End Bible Poverty Now* (YWAM Publishing: Seattle, 2017), 123.

28. Robert H. Glover, *The Bible Basis of Missions* (Moody Press: Chicago, 1946), 178.

29. If you are an adult looking for renewed purpose in putting your skills to work for the kingdom, consider the opportunities available through Mission Builders International; https://www.missionbuilders.org/.

30. Jim Stier, *His Kingdom Come* (YWAM Publishing: Seattle, 2008), 24.

31. Patrick Johnstone and Jason Mandryk, *Operation World* (Paternoster Publishing: Waynesboro, VA, 1995). See also http://www.operationworld.org.

32. See https://joshuaproject.net/pray/unreachedoftheday/app.

33. "State of the World: The Task Remaining," https://globalfrontiermissions.org/gfm-101-missions-course/state-of-the-world-the-task-remaining/ (accessed October 2018).

34. Lou Engle, *Pray! Ekballo!* (TheCall, Inc.: Pasadena, CA, 2013), 17-18. See also "TheCall" http://www.thecall.com (TheCall, Inc.: Colorado Springs).

35. Families with children or teens will love reading *The Himalayan Rescue*, from the Reel Kids Adventure Series available from YWAM Publishing. Author Dave Gustaveson wrote a fictitious story based on our real life Himalaya rescue of David and Jasmine.

36. See Marty Meyer, *Epic Faith* (YWAM Publishing: Seattle, 2016), 95-96.

37. "e3 RESOURCES: simply sharing stories," http://www.e3resources.org (accessed October 2018).

38. The Jesus Film Project App is a free download available at: https://www.jesusfilm.org/strategies-and-tools/resources/the-app.html.

39. Nik Ripkin, *The Insanity of Obedience* (B&H Publishing: Nashville, 2014), 47-48.

40. David Garrison, *Church Planting Movements,* (Wig Take Resources: Arkadelphia, AR, 2004), 21.

41. Victor John, "Movements Multiplying Movements," *Mission Frontiers* (40:1, 2018), 32-33.

42. Notice the similarity between this Gospel-confirming miracle and the one found in Luke 13:10-17.

43. We can see a biblical example of this in Acts chapter 18. Apollos was named after the Greek god Apollo, a prominent deity during the time. Apollos, however, was a fervent follower of Christ, and yet still used his Greek name. In no historical record do we see Apollos changing to a more "Christian" name. Also, nowhere do we have record of other believers requesting that he does so. In fact, Paul speaks highly of him using his Greek name in the books of 1 Corinthians and Titus.

44. Steve Smith and Stan Parks, "The War that Finally Ends," *Mission Frontiers* (40:1, 2018), 6-13.

45. David and Paul Watson, *Contagious Disciple Making,* (Thomas Nelson, Nashville: 2014).

46. James Nyman, *Stubborn Perseverance,* (Mission Network: Mount Vernon, WA, 2015).

47. Adapted from *Epic Faith* (YWAM Publishing: Seattle, 2016), 114-115.

48. Adapted from *Epic Faith* (YWAM Publishing: Seattle, 2016), 115-118.

49. See Revelation 19:11-16, 20:1-10.

50. This Gospel tract, "Are You Forgiven," is available at www.epicfaith.net.

51. For more information on this program and others like it, visit www.ywamidaho.org.

52. Ross Tooley, *Adventures in Naked Faith* (YWAM Publishing: Seattle, 1996).

53. Kel Steiner, *Adventures in Saying Yes to God,* (CreateSpace Independent Publishing Platform, 2014).

54. *Epic Faith* (YWAM Publishing: Seattle, 2016).

55. Nik Ripkin, *The Insanity of Obedience* (B&H Publishing: Nashville, 2014), 22-23.

56. This story was adapted from *Epic Faith* (YWAM Publishing: Seattle, 2016), 102-103.

57. See "Pray for the 31," https://www.go31.org.

58. William Forbush, *Foxe's Book of Martyrs* (Zondervan: Grand Rapids, 1967), 9.

59. John Piper, "A Call for Christian Risk," https://www.desiringgod.org/articles /a-call-for-christian-risk (29 May 2002, accessed October 2018).

Appendix

Figure 1

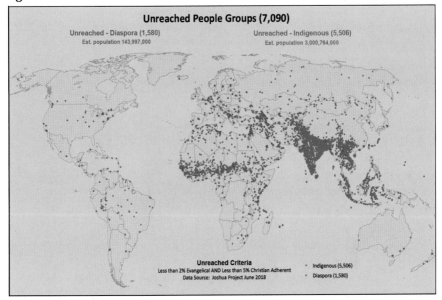

Copyright 2018 Joshua Project. Used with permission.

Figure 2

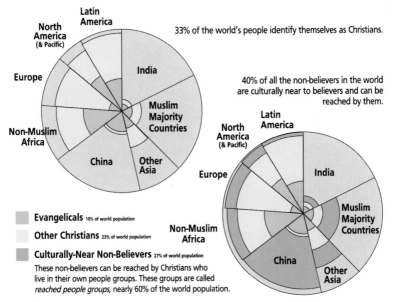

Copyright 2018 R.W. Lewis and Chris Maynard. Used with permission.

Figure 3

Foreign Missions Resource Allocation

Category	% of Foreign Missions Giving
Giving to Foreign Missions for work among already Christian groups	87%
Giving to Foreign Missions for work among people that live within reach of the Gospel but haven't responded	12%
Giving to Foreign Missions for work among unreached people groups.	1%

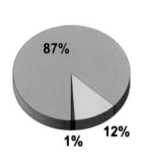

Figure 4

Understanding the Remaining Mission Task (2018)

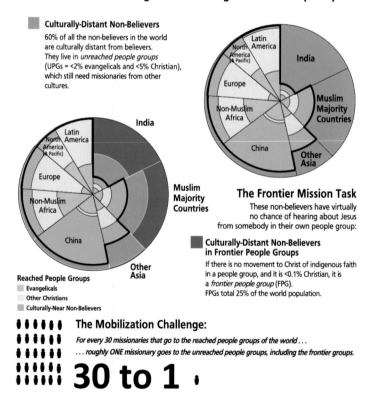

Culturally-Distant Non-Believers
60% of all the non-believers in the world are culturally distant from believers. They live in *unreached people groups* (UPGs = <2% evangelicals and <5% Christian), which still need missionaries from other cultures.

Reached People Groups
Evangelicals
Other Christians
Culturally-Near Non-Believers

The Frontier Mission Task
These non-believers have virtually no chance of hearing about Jesus from somebody in their own people group:

Culturally-Distant Non-Believers in Frontier People Groups
If there is no movement to Christ of indigenous faith in a people group, and it is <0.1% Christian, it is a *frontier people group* (FPG). FPGs total 25% of the world population.

The Mobilization Challenge:
For every 30 missionaries that go to the reached people groups of the world . . .
. . . roughly ONE missionary goes to the unreached people groups, including the frontier groups.

30 to 1

JOIN THE FINAL PUSH

24:14 IS A GLOBAL MOVEMENT

PRAYING AND WORKING TOGETHER TO START KINGDOM MOVEMENT ENGAGEMENTS IN EVERY UNREACHED PEOPLE AND PLACE BY 2025.

"This gospel of the kingdom will be preached as a testimony to all nations, and then the end will come."
–MATTHEW 24:14

Reaching the Unreached

We believe that kingdom movements are the biblical and only viable approach to finishing the Great Commission.

Church Planting Movements

We see God work in the world through movements - we are joining Him in launching kingdom movements in every unreached people group and place.

24:14

Urgency

We are catalyzing these kingdom movements with wartime urgency to see every people group engaged by December 31, 2025 - no matter the cost.

Collaboration

We believe that it will take a full representation of the Body of Christ to fulfill the Great Commission, and seek to be open-handed with information and resources.

JOIN THE MOVEMENT & MAKE THE COMMITMENT

www.2414now.net/connect

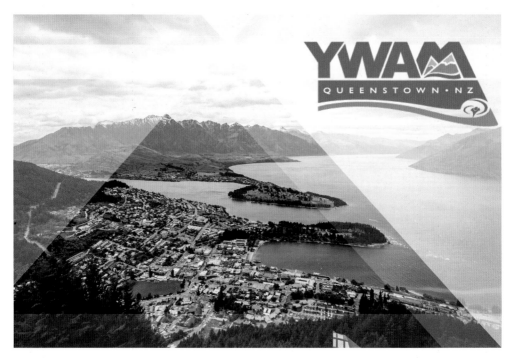

Join a vibrant community of believers in stunning Queenstown, New Zealand. Experience transformation and revelation in a DTS, or dive deeper into the Bible and Evangelism through our Second-Level Schools.

TRAINING

DISCIPLESHIP TRAINING SCHOOLS

Arise | Classic | Creative Arts | Extreme | Media | Prayer & Compassion | Skate | Ski & Snowboard | Sports | Worship

SECOND-LEVEL SCHOOLS

Discipleship Bible School

School of Evangelism

Get to know God's word in a deeper way during a DBS. Discover a new passion and hunger for the Bible as you spend time diving into it.

Join an SOE and discover boldness and a renewed desire to bring the Gospel to the world. Learn the why and how behind effective, powerful evangelism.

www ywamqueenstown.com   @ywamqueenstown
                          @ywamqueenstown

One day thousands will be praying for him.
Will you be one of them?

Get the Unreached of the Day app.   JoshuaProject.net

www.ywamphoenix.com

JOIN US!

Pray for the 31
Largest Frontier People Groups

One fourth of all people alive on the planet today live in Frontier People Groups. These are people groups with virtually no contact with Christ-followers, and no sign yet of a gospel movement bringing God's promised blessing. The few who do identify as Christians among them are 0.1% or less (one in a thousand) of their people group.

Until God intervenes, the families in these peoples will live and die...

- without ever knowing a believer.
- without ever being prayed for by name.
- without knowing the Father who longs to embrace and bless them.

And yet, in our day God is moving.

- Among other people groups, Acts-like gospel movements have been doubling in number and size every five years since the late 1990s.
- Global prayer networks are now focusing united prayer for these 31 largest Frontier People Groups.

Contains the information you need to pray strategically for these groups!

There are thousands of Frontier People Groups, but half the population of all those living in Frontier People Groups live in the largest 31 of these groups.

Visit **Go31**.org

- Get your no-cost digital prayer guide (English/Spanish)
- Request a no-cost print review copy (English only)
- Order a quantity to share with others
- Check for other translations (many in process)
- Join the effort to bring God's blessing to these Frontier People Groups

Will you join a

MOVEMENT?

Help us support, encourage, and pray for church planters who are on the front lines of the Mission.

harvestfrontiers.org

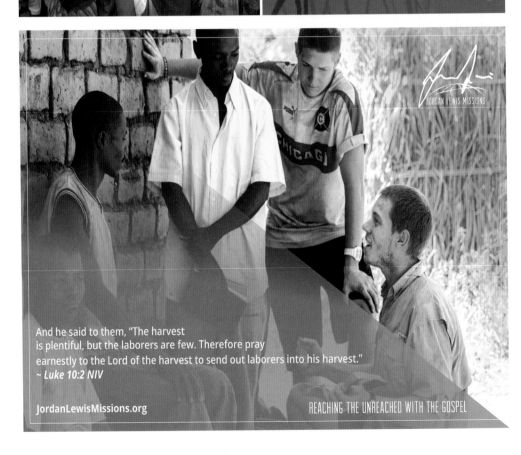

And he said to them, "The harvest is plentiful, but the laborers are few. Therefore pray earnestly to the Lord of the harvest to send out laborers into his harvest."
~ *Luke 10:2 NIV*

JordanLewisMissions.org

REACHING THE UNREACHED WITH THE GOSPEL

MISSION
ADVENTURES

SHORT TERM OUTREACH FOR GROUPS

MISSION ADVENTURES IS FULL SERVICE

Our experienced Youth With A Mission staff will take care of the details.
We cover all the bases—food, housing, transportation, ministry planning,
translation, supplies and everything else so you can focus on your team.
You show up with your students, we'll handle the rest.

MISSION ADVENTURES MEANS TRAINING

You won't go unprepared. Our experienced missionaries will equip you
and your team with proven tools so you can express the Gospel across
cultures. Not only will we prepare your hands, our camp-like training
will prepare your hearts for all that God intends to do through and in
your group.

MISSION ADVENTURES MEANS SPIRITUAL GROWTH

In serving others, your kids can become who they are intended to be.
Jesus teaches us that when we lose ourselves for His sake, that's when
we really find out who we are. When you take your group on a Mission
Adventures outreach, your kids will lose themselves in serving others.
They'll discover what they're made of and they will grow.

MISSIONADVENTURES.NET

A Ministry of Youth With A Mission

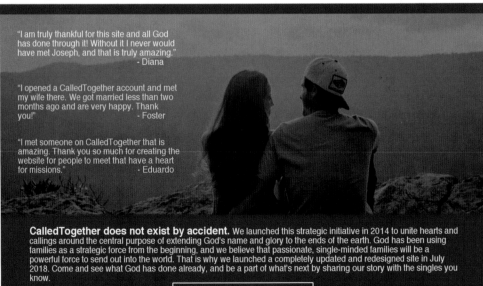

YOU CAN

Whatever stage of life, you can join the Great Commission through short-term service. With over 40 years of experience, MBI can help connect you to serve alongside YWAM ministries in over 180 nations!

I came here on my **gap year** and haven't regretted it. I will go home a changed person with a much bigger, God-centered scope for life.

We **retired**, bought an RV and serve YWAM locations as we travel around the US. We've made many friends in this new season of usefulness.

Serving overseas as a **family** has expanded our children's world view and strengthened our family tremendously in the Lord.

Our church **group** came and it has been amazing to serve the people here. We came to be a blessing but we're seeing how God has blessed us through our experience.

MISSION BUILDERS INTERNATIONAL
Toll Free: 866.844.2683
Web: www.missionbuilders.org
Email: team@missionbuilders.org

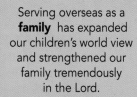
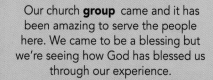

GO & SERVE.

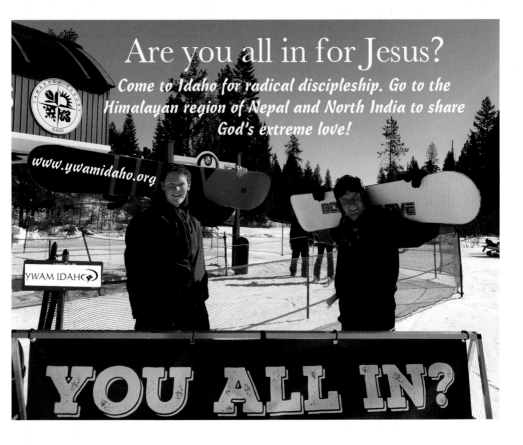

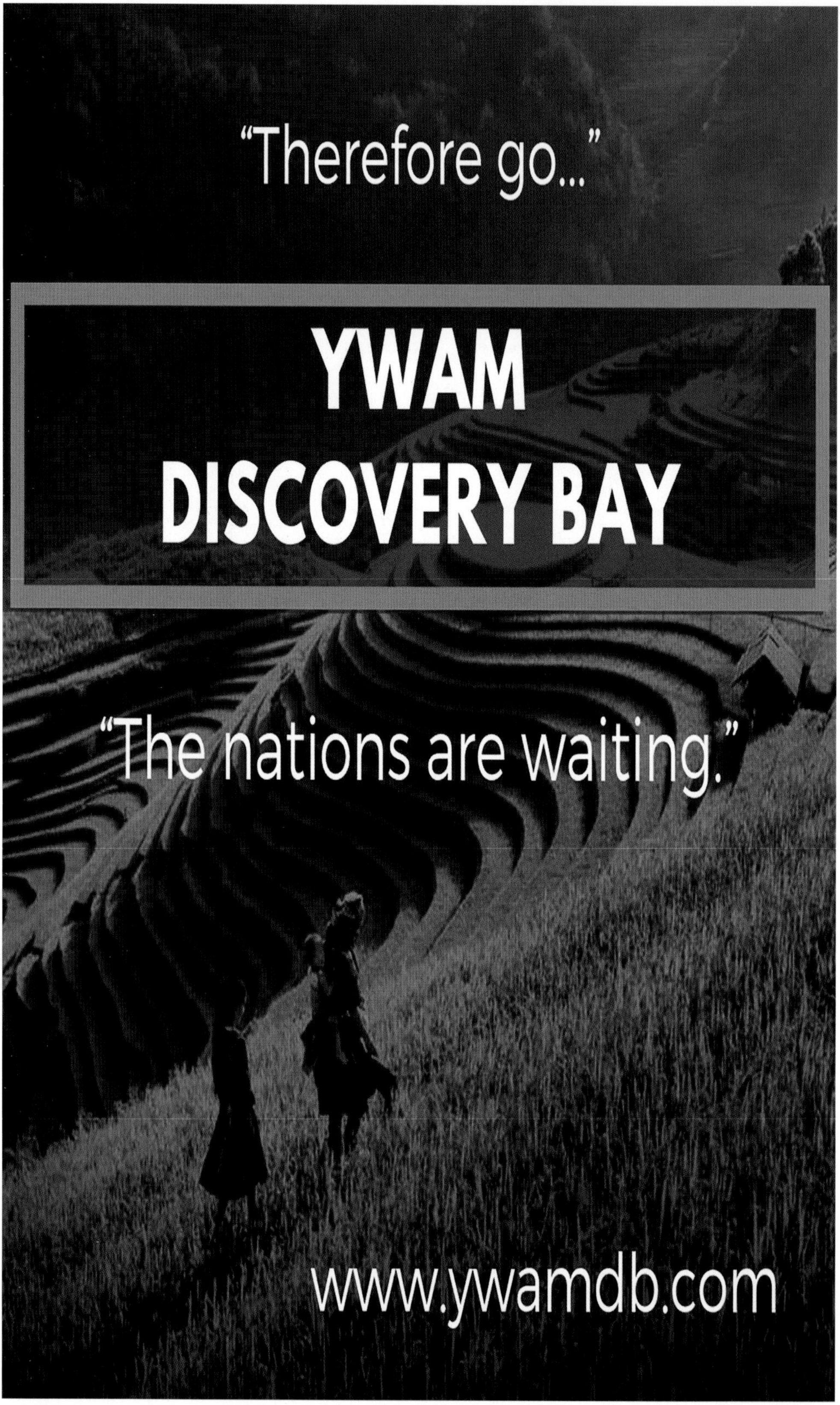
"Therefore go..."
YWAM
DISCOVERY BAY
"The nations are waiting."
www.ywamdb.com

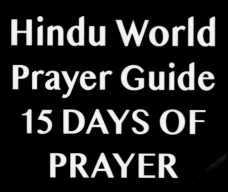

Hindu World Prayer Guide
15 DAYS OF PRAYER
2019 DATES
20 OCT - 3 NOV

An Annual Prayer Movement Of
Christians Learning About And
Praying For The Hindu World

For More Information Please Visit
www.pray15days.org

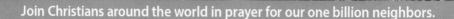

Join Christians around the world in prayer for our one billion neighbors.

Join the Fight!

Send Pioneers
Pursue Truth
Provide Hospitality

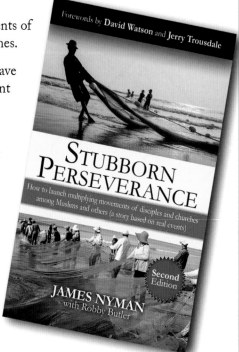

ywam

Frontier Missions
South Asia

Want to be a part of empowering Indigenous Church Planters?

In South Asia, YWAM Indigenous Church Planters face tremendous challenges when raising financial support. We train Indigenous Church planters with the fundraising skills necessary to help them raise support from their communities. To encourage them to continue raising their support and to honor their hard work, we also provide limited matching funds.

MULTIPLYING DISCIPLES
AMONG THE LEAST, LAST AND LOST
YWAM Frontier Missions
will train you how
to start movements
of passionate Jesus followers.
ywam
Frontier Missions
ywamfm.org

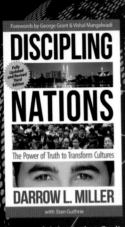

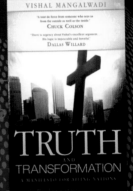

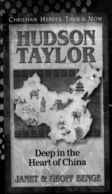

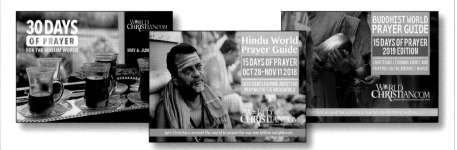